My Wake Up Fall

How landing on my face taught me
how to stand on my feet

JOELLE KANTOR

BALBOA.PRESS

A DIVISION OF HAY HOUSE

Balboa Press books may be ordered through booksellers or by contacting:

Balboa Press
A Division of Hay House
1663 Liberty Drive
Bloomington, IN 47403
www.balboapress.com
844-682-1282

Because of the dynamic nature of the Internet, any web addresses or links contained in this book may have changed since publication and may no longer be valid. The views expressed in this work are solely those of the author and do not necessarily reflect the views of the publisher, and the publisher hereby disclaims any responsibility for them.

The author of this book does not dispense medical advice or prescribe the use of any technique as a form of treatment for physical, emotional, or medical problems without the advice of a physician, either directly or indirectly. The intent of the author is only to offer information of a general nature to help you in your quest for emotional and spiritual well-being. In the event you use any of the information in this book for yourself, which is your constitutional right, the author and the publisher assume no responsibility for your actions.

Any people depicted in stock imagery provided by Getty Images are models, and such images are being used for illustrative purposes only. Certain stock imagery © Getty Images.

Print information available on the last page.

ISBN: 978-1-9822-6550-2 (sc)
ISBN: 978-1-9822-6552-6 (hc)
ISBN: 978-1-9822-6551-9 (e)

Library of Congress Control Number: 2021904999

Balboa Press rev. date: 03/26/2021

"It is often during the most challenging times where there is the greatest opportunity to redefine yourself." ~Shilagh Mirgain, Ph.D

"And the time came when the risk to remain tight in a bud was more painful than the risk it took to blossom." ~Anais Nin

CONTENTS

DEDICATION

To my loving family - Doron, Sammy, Nate and Kennedy - I could not have survived the storm without your strength, courage and compassion. I love you all to the moon and back.

And to anyone who is personally struggling with a trauma or helping a loved one through theirs: Stay the course, trust the process, and choose to live in acceptance of whatever is meant to be. While the reason is not always clear, everything will always work out as it is supposed to.

"I'm thankful for my struggle because without it I wouldn't have stumbled across my strength." ~Alex Elle

INTRODUCTION

One of the most common questions people have ever pondered is, "What is the meaning of life?" Birds seem to just know it. I have always admired the way they fly through life so effortlessly, with such ease and grace. They gather seeds for the winter, forage worms for their young and fly south to follow the sun, joyously chirping all the while. Our answers to "what is the meaning of life?" are infinite: Love, joy, family, learning, growth, being of service and so on. I believe these answers are all important facets of life that we would be privileged to experience, but for me, the ultimate meaning of life is: *purpose.* We don't exist merely to exist. We come here to discover our own, unique purposes. For some people that is an easy task. It comes to them early on, and clicks right away. Others may not find their purpose until later in life. And some of us must go through deep, dark struggles and repair badly broken wings for our individual purposes to be revealed. Whatever the case, I believe we are all very important beings with very meaningful and unique missions; just as our missions are as critical as those of the birds in the sky.

This book is a collection of memories from my life, during my period of greatest struggle, from 2014-2017, after I sustained my fourth and most life-altering head injury, which became the most life-altering one. Much of what I went through was extremely terrifying, disturbing and agonizing. The twenty-plus health professionals I visited called my condition a "mystery illness," and were stumped about how to help me. Had I realized then that all of my physical anguish came from numerous and exacerbated traumas to my brain, I could have avoided the seemingly countless, insufferable appointments that I went to, trying to find relief from "healers." As I came to learn, head injuries, especially compounding ones take their own time to heal - in my case, three years. Instead of looking outside of myself, the experience I went through taught me how to look within and be my own healer; how to find the courage and patience I needed in order to overcome my suffering. I came to discover that the healers I encountered along my journey were not supposed to "heal me," but were people who would awaken my own ability to heal myself. The guidance I received along my three year path helped me to mend my own injured wings.

I spent innumerable moments during those three years searching high and low for any semblance of relief, from any resource I could find. I was in a perpetual state of fight or flight, which caused my thinking to constantly fluctuate from hopeful to dire. Was I doubtful of the sporadic positive insights that I received in the midst of my extreme adrenalized state? Absolutely I was - every single long, distressing day; but something kept reminding me that those uplifting messages were sent from The Universe, and that I must stay focused on those messages and not on my excruciating physical condition. Even during the hell I was going through, I also had a strong sense of growth, discovery and, yes, PURPOSE. That strong sense of purpose enabled me to visualize being on the other side of my darkness, finally enlightened and eager to fly.

Whenever I felt like I was at the end of my rope, I somehow convinced myself that the timeline of my experience was like getting the flu, as one might feel achy, weak and uncomfortable, but also would expect that in seven to ten days, they'd be living life like their illness never happened. I kept praying that each new day would be the first of those seven to ten "flu days" and that afterward, I would be on the mend. I played that hopeful visualization game every day for three seemingly endless, agonizing years. It felt like I was lost in the ocean, and my suffering came in tidal waves that I had to tackle one after another. Admittedly, I often reached points where I didn't think I would ever again experience that "winning feeling" of being fully engaged in life.

Despite the pain I endured, I kept believing that everything I was going through was part of my migration towards my purpose. I feel blessed to have had a team of patient, compassionate and strong family members, friends and professionals who were never going to give up on my recovery, no matter how challenging it got... and it got *very* challenging. If they believed my life was worth fighting for, I had to believe it myself. The love that I was given helped me to work through my injury, and also enabled me to heal much of my past emotional pain and traumas, which I had unknowingly locked away, deep inside.

And now here, on the other side of the abyss, I feel grateful and elated to have discovered *me* and to be on this journey, free of the once-constant pain and discomfort I lived with for so long. I feel grateful every single day that I am able to experience life after that perilous period; and I believe that my PURPOSE is guiding others to arrive at a similar place. If my story will help just *one* other person find hope through their trials of life, I will feel fulfilled. I pray that my small contribution in the world will make a world of difference for someone.

The Universe will sometimes literally knock you on your ass, or in my case my face, to get you to show up and deal with the things that are in your way, so you can get back on your feet, realize your PURPOSE and even learn to soar.

I was thrown down hard and fast, with a side of whiplash, which is why I call this memoir MY WAKE UP FALL.

"Your vision will become clear only when you can look into your own heart. Who looks outside, dreams: Who looks inside, awakes." ~Carl Jung

PROLOGUE

The title, "My Wake Up Fall," came to me like a bolt of lightning, within the first month or two of my three-year odyssey through hell, as I lay on my floor shaking, trying to at least find some meaning for what I was going through, since I could not find any solace. Perhaps if I understood the destination, I could press through to survive the journey.

I recognized that I was the observer of my experience, as my spiritual teachers would say, though I could not escape also being the main character in my real life horror film, since the pain I was in was far too intense to simply observe. It was all so surreal, like a movie, which is why the following chapters are called "scenes." And, like any good flick, I have also included "bloopers" for your reading entertainment. Hey, every storm cloud has a silver lining.

The following scenes and poems are excerpts from and descriptions of the trauma I experienced, and my journey towards healing and reconnecting with my soul in the process.

SCENE 1
Off My Path

I t was eight in the morning and everyone had gone off to work and school. The house was silent and I was alone, feeling fatigued and foggy. I was stuck in a rut of judgment, comparison, envy and lack of self-confidence. In summary: I felt crappy. As long as I could remember, I saw myself as not good enough and as lacking the accomplishments that society considered I should have acquired by that point in my life. I was hoping that some exercise in the fresh air would clear my head. I started jogging on the sidewalk, the sun beaming in my eyes, and I remember feeling lost. At that time in my life, I thought that the only way to feel light, free and happy was to get my life to appear as if I had it all together on the outside, according to societal standards. That meant that all my relationships should look a certain way. All my belongings should be at a certain standard. I needed a career to prove I was worthy... and because I thought I didn't have any of those things that society deemed important, I felt lost. Little did I know how lost I was about to become. As I drifted sluggishly down the sidewalk, I can remember feeling so much dissatisfaction with my life. I felt frustrated and guilty for comparing myself to and judging others for so long. How was I going to make my life "exciting" and "perfect" being in so much judgment all the time? I certainly had a fantasy of how... if only I had *this* or *that*, I would be satisfied. I was tragically far off of my authentic path, and The Universe was about to WAKE MY ASS UP!

I decided to turn down a street I had never been on before. I was still in such a funk and not paying much attention to my surroundings, and then *it* happened. I tripped. I hit the ground hard and fast. My head whiplashed intensely as my hands and knees barely caught my fall. There I was, my chin half an inch from the sidewalk, my knees and hands burning, and my body in shock. I jumped up in embarrassment, looked around to see if anyone saw me and tried to play it cool, just in case anyone did. My insecurities got the best of me. I even called my husband, Doron, to crack a joke at my own clumsiness. I was always told how hard I was on myself, and now looking back at my reaction to my fall, I can see it crystal clear. I felt so stupid. At that stage of my life, I felt lost with no purpose, and I didn't know how to fix it. Then, to top it all off, I was injured. I hobbled my way home, cleaned up my wounds and went about my day.

A couple of days after my fall, I started to feel progressively more dizzy and out of balance. It felt hauntingly familiar, like the insidious claws of vertigo. I had experienced extremely bad vertigo years before, so I was familiar with the feeling and believed it would eventually fade away. The reverse happened. It got worse and worse and worse.

My son Nate's bar mitzvah was coming up, and there was so much to do in preparation for it, in addition to my daily responsibilities of taking care of our household - three kids, a dog, a cat and a husband. In the Jewish religion, the bar mitzvah is a ritual that marks the milestone of a boy or girl turning thirteen years of age, where they are seen as an "adult" in their tradition. Jewish children begin preparing for this important event in their lives at around ten years old. On the Sabbath closest to the individual's birthday, they lead their community in a religious service by reading from the Torah and helping to conduct the congregation in prayer. The week before the bar mitzvah, I couldn't sleep at all. I had insomnia, which made it excruciatingly challenging for me to function during the day. Everyone thought I was just nervous about the event, which was fast approaching, but that was not the case at all. Something else was happening inside of me, beyond mere nerves. My brain was injured for the fourth time.

When I was twenty-eight years old, I played on a coed softball team. I was playing first base during one of our practices, and was unaware of a fastball coming towards me from the second baseman. As I turned to look in that direction, the ball smacked me in the right eye and I fell to the ground, fast. It struck my face so hard that it split the skin next to my eye, requiring me to go to the ER where I received several stitches. I had quite a nice shiner for the next several weeks. A few years later, while inner-tubing behind a boat, I was thrown up into the air. When I slammed back down onto the surface of the water, I was suddenly struck extremely hard in the face by my inner-tube, like a boxer who never saw the knockout punch coming. The blow was hard enough that it caused my nose to bleed. It was so hard that I developed temporary hearing loss in my right ear, which later morphed into tinnitus. The next day, I began experiencing severe vertigo symptoms. I felt like the world was spinning. As a result of the dizziness, I couldn't open my eyes without feeling nauseous. I was forced to stay in bed for six weeks with my eyes closed. My third head injury occurred while playing coed soccer. A burly man ran towards me at lightning speed and flattened me like a pancake. My head hit the ground forcefully. It took quite some time for me to be able to stand up again. I was sore and fatigued for weeks afterward. Then, with my fourth head injury, signs of compounded damage began emerging, over which I had no control.

The mounting physical effects of my injury only added to the gravity of my situation; to how little I could participate in my son's bar mitzvah. Nate's milestone was a once-in-a-lifetime occasion, and I wanted to be present and feeling well. Due to the burning, buzzing and throbbing sensations in my brain, my lack of sleep and my inability to stand upright without my symptoms flaring, I ended up missing his Friday night Shabbat dinner. I was heartbroken. The bar mitzvah celebration begins on Friday evening, a few minutes before sunset, and ends after the appearance of three stars in the sky on Saturday evening. Candles are lit and prayers are recited over the sacred bread (challah) and wine. Family and loved ones gather to acknowledge the emerging adult being honored. For so many years I had imagined proudly celebrating Nate's achievement from beginning to end. Instead, I missed the Shabbat dinner because I was at home, suffering. My son's monumental weekend was not turning out the way that I had envisioned it would. I felt deflated, disheartened and devastated. I was also enduring virtually intolerable physical symptoms. My life was in a tailspin.

Saturday morning, the day of my son's bar mitzvah, arrived and I hadn't slept for four nights straight... *at all.* I had made appointments for my daughter, Kennedy, and myself to get our hair and makeup done, and I felt like I had been hit by a truck. I didn't think there would be enough concealer in the artist's kit to hide the bags under my eyes. Feeling so awful was another disappointment, as I was really looking forward to enjoying the special "girl time" together with my young daughter. I forced myself to get up and out the front door of my house, and we headed to the mall. I remember sitting in the artist's chair with my eyes closed as the gal did my makeup. My head was spinning, and I felt extreme irritability, with discomfort running through me, as though someone was wringing my brain out like a wet towel. My frontal lobe felt like an angry toddler was squeezing it like putty and stabbing it like a voodoo doll. I was so exhausted from lack of sleep, that I could barely hold myself upright. Somehow I made it through the application, but then I was wondering how I would make it through the service and get up in front of family and friends to give my congratulatory speech to my son. On the outside, no one could tell that anything was wrong - typical me (I guess that under-eye concealer did work), but I was desperately struggling through family pictures. I began to think it might be better if I passed on my speech, but when the time came, I pushed through, knowing I would never have that opportunity again, and presented my special wishes to Nate. Apparently, I did a great job and was still undercover, hiding the excruciating reality of the extent of my pain.

As I walked into the banquet room where the party was being held, I remember feeling very light-headed, as if the ground was moving under my feet. Seismic shifts shook my body. It felt like forever weaving my way through the congratulating guests en route to the buffet. I knew I had to get some food in me. I felt like I was going to faint. The glaring lights and blaring music coming from the DJ booth were overly stimulating, and I became panicky. Why was this happening to me on this special night? I was very disappointed. I hurried to find my husband, Doron, and he escorted me downstairs to get some air. My mom and stepdad followed him down to check on me. The anxiety I felt was through-the-roof, and they all encouraged me to go to the ER. I knew I was going to miss Nate's slide show and cake, but I really had no choice at that point. I desperately needed help.

We waited in the ER for hours before anyone got to me. It was torture. All I wanted to do was sleep. My body couldn't take it anymore. I wasn't a big fan of medication, but at that point, I begged to be knocked out and put fast asleep. At that point I had surrendered to the pain. The ER doctor gave me some meds and sent me home. I went to my mom's house, and was *finally* able to fall asleep, but little did I know that was the beginning of a horrible nightmare.

....

"Something will grow from all you are going through. And it will be you." ~Unknown

....

SCENE 2
Sympathetic Saint Kelly

"One of the most important things you can do on this earth is to let people know they are not alone." ~Shannon L. Adler

My downward spiral and the insomnia continued for months. I would toss and turn during the night and not be able to function during the day. The anxiety was constant and excruciating, like wearing a shock collar that was turned to the highest setting. All I could do was cry from the discomfort. I felt like I was walking through quicksand and sinking, never able to get my footing on solid ground. My brain was wobbly, buzzy and creating sensations that I would have never dreamed could exist. No one understood me, they could only observe my suffering. At that point, everyone was focused on me and trying to find a solution to help alleviate my pain, suggesting, "Try this, try that." Of course, their advice came from a place of love, but all the advising became overwhelming for me. I just wanted it all to end. I did not need that kind of attention, and I didn't know how to make it stop! My husband helped me through endless anxiety attacks, came home from work early, missed work altogether... and all of that created even more stress for me, as I didn't want to take him away from his clinic. The condition I was in left me feeling very fragile, nervous, and frightened. I was unable to care for myself. Being alone created much worry for me. The severity of my symptoms also caused my husband to feel concerned about my safety when I was home alone without supervision. He knew I was at a precipice in life; he saw that the acute agony I was experiencing was too much for me to endure.

There were many times, day and night, when Doron would take me for a drive, sometimes for hours at a time, as riding in the car seemed to calm my sensations a bit. He would also rub my back almost every night to help me relax so that I could, by the grace of God, perhaps doze off briefly. A friend of mine even said that Doron deserved the "Husband of the Year" award three years in a row. I viewed our situation as the epitome of the phrase, "for better or for worse." I don't think either of us could imagine our predicament being much worse than it was, though. After many months of Doron missing entire days of work, sporadically, the time eventually came when he could not stay home with me any longer, as he had a clinic to run. He asked his office manager, Kelly (bless her heart) to start caring for me so that he could go back to work.

Kelly stopped working at Doron's office and started working as my caretaker, while fielding office calls from our house. She would drive an hour and a half, only to experience tsunamis of tears, inconsolable complaining, panicking, stressing and more panicking from me, all day long. Then she would drive another hour and a half back home, wake up and do it all over again each day. She definitely must have been living for the weekends. The amazing part about Kelly was that she could actually handle me and what I was going through. She knew how to calm me down, the best I could be calmed down, by encouraging me to focus on objects in the room to distract me from my symptoms, as well as by rubbing my feet and talking calmly to me in a way that gave me hope and strength. She'd remind me, "Joelle you are a fighter, you can overcome anything. Inhale... exhale..." She had a confidence that inspired me to trust that I would eventually be well again. There were even days when we had some good laughs. I always appreciated those laughs, even though the chuckles didn't take away the intensity of what I was feeling.

One cold and snowy afternoon, Kelly asked me to walk around my yard barefoot. The intention was to get my focus out of my head and onto my feet. It was very cold outside, but I managed to do as she asked. It was definitely a distraction, but again, not a cure for my symptoms. "A" for effort though, Kelly. Eventually, my feet felt numb, and I ran to the door to get back inside our warm house. Unfortunately, the door was locked. My dog had been jumping on the door wanting to join us, and had inadvertently locked us out. Even under the shitty circumstances, I had to admit the situation was pretty darn funny. I was barefoot, in the snow, freezing, with a throbbing head injury. "Good one, God," is what I thought. Kelly started checking for unlocked windows, to no avail. My husband is ultra-concerned about safety, even adopting our two 150 pound Boerboel Mastiff dogs, Bauer and Thunder, as part of our alarm system, so nope, there were no unlocked windows to be found on the ground floor. There was a tree outside my son's window, and a balcony there, too. We thought his window could possibly be open, since he was a teenage boy and had to aerate his musky room, where both he and his pungent ferrets dwelled, so Kelly started climbing the tree. It was quite a funny sight. Doron called her cell phone while she was mid-climb, and she answered the call! Watching her trying to talk and hang on to the tree at the same time, while hysterically laughing, was a sight to behold. I just remember thinking, "What the hell is going on?" and, "I hope I can actually have a good laugh when I am all better, and can genuinely feel happy again."

Kelly helped encourage me to stay hopeful by sending me this quote on a particularly challenging day, which sustained me through some of my darkest times:

"In case no one told you today: You're beautiful. You're loved. You're needed. You're alive for a reason. You're stronger than you think. You're going to get through this. I'm glad you're alive. Don't give up."

....

"Let us be grateful to people who make us happy. They are the charming gardeners who make our souls blossom." ~Marcel Proust

....

RELIEF

Each day I wake to a wobbly brain,
Buzzy head, it's always the same.

My heart is heavy, so sad, so deep,
Then I break into my morning weep.

I push myself up, my body so weak
And pray I will find the relief that I seek.

The days are long while the symptoms run wild,
My mind and body fatigue;
The process makes me so tired.

The anxiety is so strong, adrenaline too;
My poor nervous system doesn't know what to do.

My brain is busy wondering when this will be done;
And I can't stop thinking about the day when I've won.

But it's not just me who seeks the relief that I do,
My wonderful family, they need relief, too.

How heartbreaking and sad to watch a loved one go through hell,
Especially when you feel helpless and just want them to be well.

All the stress and concern my family must take,
Extra chores and planning, we all need a break.

Please send us the relief and answers we desire,
So we can all celebrate life and put out this fire.

SCENE 3
Desperately Seeking Relief

The next few months were filled with doctor appointments, where I would have to repeat my story for the nth time, and lying around my house, miserable, crying relentlessly. One day, my curious and insightful son, Nate, asked me, "Mom, where do all of your tears come from?" He made a great point. It felt like I had already cried an ocean of tears, and they just kept pouring forth each day. At least some part of my body was working properly - my tear ducts.

Dr. Jeanette, D.C., was the first person we called for expert assistance after my fall. In addition to being a chiropractor, Dr. Jeanette had twenty-plus years of experience in nutritional counseling. My husband had met her years earlier at a seminar where she was a featured speaker. He was very interested in her work and decided to make an appointment with her. Dr. Jeanette had actually helped me with some health issues prior to my fall. She was able to help me get off the medication that I was on at the time, and I consequently felt better than I had in years.

I stayed late at her office many a night, while she spent *hours* conducting tests and protocols to try and help me find some relief. She was a vital mentor in my story, as she stuck with me through it all. She would allow my kids and me to call her anytime, and she talked me through many panicky moments and uncontrollable sobbing breakdowns. Jeanette and her staff made me feel so comfortable in whatever state I needed to be in, without judgment. They did whatever they could to help us find answers. Jeanette's support was above and beyond our expectations. What an amazing soul. While I'm sure Dr. Jeanette's nutritional guidance was beneficial on some level (and I know that her protocols have helped many people over the years), simply changing my diet did not alleviate my symptoms; and my nightmarish descent continued.

Little did I know then that the next three years would be filled with pokes, prods, scans, pills, therapies, drives, flights, appointments, anxiety attacks, breakdowns and suicidal thoughts. Sometimes it's better not to know what's coming than to know that you're about to go through hell. There is a reason we can't see the future.

> *"Sometimes life is about the ability to believe*
> *in where you are going even when you're*
> *not sure what lies ahead."* ~Unknown

SCENE 4
Out of Patience

As the months painstakingly passed by, slow as molasses, my anxiety reached full throttle. In my anguished state, my ability to function disintegrated. I would find myself lying on the floor, staring at the ceiling, barely able to move, feeling trapped in my own body. I found myself constantly asking, "Why? Why the hell is this happening? What is the point of all of this?" There was a conflict raging inside of me between strength and fear. I heard a part of me cheering myself on, and another part doubting my ability to make it through. The battle created more fuel for my fiery cortisol, adrenaline and out-of-whack hormonal levels. I felt myself moving further away from any type of balance or harmony, until I could only describe my existence as torturous. I became a prisoner in my own body and I couldn't get out! To compound matters, I had way too much time to think and to stress about being an inconvenience to my husband and kids. My friends and family were curious about my well-being, but didn't know what to make of my situation, or how to act. I worried about what others were saying, and whether they would support or abandon me during my most crucial time of need. I felt like I urgently wanted to shift something, or, better yet, to make the whole situation go away… but everything continued to drag on. Time was *not* on my side.

My life became a monotonous Groundhog Day of moving from room to room, constantly seeking a change of scenery. My mind wanted to get up and go, but my body wasn't feeling the same, so I had to stay still. I felt like I could empathize with people who had some kind of paralysis of the body (though their minds may be high functioning) and with people in a coma who could hear their loved ones all around them, but could not respond. The symptoms I experienced daily raged out of control, and it took every last bit of strength I had to fight through the agony. I was exhausted by the end of each day, but could barely even sleep. Some Higher Power was forcing me to have major *patience*... patience like I have never had to muster in all my life - as a mother of three, a preschool teacher, a director of a children's sports program... nothing compared to the patience I needed to have with myself at that time. It would have been one thing to deal with my conditions if I were at all rested, but let's not forget Ms. Insomnia who haunted me, and who wouldn't *leave me the fuck alone*! You know how they say, "Time flies when you're having fun?" Well, I discovered the opposite to be true on the other side: Time *barely moves* when you are intensely distressed. So, after each super long, drawn out, disturbing and almost unbearable day, I would then toss and turn throughout the night, becoming more weepy, frustrated, angry and disappointed. I remembered reading a quote online by Joyce Meyer which read, "Patience is not the ability to wait, but the ability to keep a good attitude while waiting." Beautiful concept. Easier said than done.

Because everyone, including myself, felt so helpless with regard to how to solve my problems, we would spend much of the days researching new doctors and the latest healing techniques to help me get some relief. This is where the "fun" really began. NOT. Week after week, month after month and dollar upon dollar, I was driven and even flown to appointment after appointment, where I would pray to finally "be saved." I had to tell my history and story over and over and over again to each new practitioner and shaman. It was getting really old, beating the drum of my tragedies, and worse yet, I was not finding any reprieve. I was so over it. That frustrating search for relief, in itself, caused me even more worry and anxiety.

I remember on so many car rides feeling as though I was a prisoner trapped behind bars yearning to be free and being so envious of those around me, even strangers, just for being able to walk down the street by themselves or drive their cars. The most simple actions were so far out of reach for me. I would think to myself, "No matter what is going on in their lives, they clearly aren't suffering from the unbearable symptoms that I am experiencing." The battle inside me would rage, "Stop feeling sorry for yourself... Stop comparing yourself to others... Stop being so negative..." Then I'd try to pep-talk myself out of the negative spiral saying, "You got this... This is your journey... There is a reason for all of this... You will get through this... Stay strong..." This constant self-talk battle was mentally draining, on top of all of the physical and emotional turmoil I was experiencing.

And it would continue like that, day after day, week after week, month after month, for three long years. In the big picture you could say (and some people did say to me), that three years is nothing; but let me be the first to tell you, it was a *long-ass time.*

••

"The moment when you want to quit, is the moment when you need to keep pushing." ~Unknown

••

SCENE 5
Thanksgiving Nightmare

"Things might not always go as planned, but they'll always end up as they should." ~Unknown

While some people may find preparing for a huge family feast a total pain in the ass, I wished that I could participate in that drama when I no longer could. I realized during my debilitated state how important it was not to take anything for granted. Thanksgiving is one of my favorite holidays. It's based around family, delicious food, and an opportunity to focus on what we have to be grateful for in our lives. Eating apple pie a' la mode is another one of my favorite parts of the holiday. Unfortunately, I didn't have the opportunity to partake in any part of what I love about Thanksgiving because Thanksgiving 2014 *sucked*. It was by far the worst Thanksgiving I have ever experienced. To start, I sadly was not feeling up to joining our wild and crazy (in the most loving way) family for the festivities that year. My husband refused to leave me alone at home (bless his heart - "through thick and thin"), so our kids were picked up by some of our family members for the day. I called my dad to wish him a Happy Thanksgiving and ended up in tears. I wanted so badly to be well and celebrating with family but instead was in so much distress. I had a dire need for people to understand what I was experiencing and yet there was no possible way to make that happen. Just like everyone else who tried to console me in my times of distress, I could hear the sadness, worry and helplessness in his voice. Not sure what to say to me in the midst of my over-the-phone breakdown, my dad handed the phone to my stepmom. She is always willing to step up when a family member is in crisis.

Despite having a feast to finish preparing, my stepmom asked me a couple of times if she could come and get me, and either take me to her house or to the ER to try and get to the bottom of my pain, as she put it. Though I attempted to decline her considerate offers, not wanting to take her away from her cooking and family time, she finally convinced me to let her pick me up and take me to the emergency room. I felt hopeful that she would make sure we really did get the answers we needed. As usual, at the ER, we played the waiting game in the waiting room before getting called back. They asked me more questions, took more tests... and we waited. My stepmom asked them if they could give me something to alleviate my symptoms, but nothing they gave me worked. I was also very concerned about taking meds due to the unpleasant experiences I had with them in the past, and the frightening side-effects they caused. For whatever reason, my body seemed to respond to medications with an adverse reaction every time. On several past occasions, I had taken medicine that was meant to relax and sedate me, but instead had me pacing all night while my heart felt like it was going to burst out of my chest. After taking the medication, I ended up feeling more anxious than I had felt before taking the pill.

After hours of waiting, my results came back "all normal." This was both relieving and frustrating at the same time. I was glad nothing serious was showing up; however, I did not feel "normal" in the least, so what the hell was going on? I left the hospital that Thanksgiving Day, answerless and just as desperate.

I was able to get my hands on a quarter of a Xanax, which I hoped would take the edge off until we could get to a new doctor. Holy cow! That quarter pill made everything slow down, made my eyes begin to water, and the yawning became non-stop. I think I even remember giggling with relief. I decided that Xanax would be my new drug, and it would make everything much better. I must just have chronic anxiety that was never diagnosed, and now I had a cure. More hope was beginning to appear... or so I thought.

"The only thing you can really control is how you react to the things out of your control." ~Bassam Tarazi

SCENE 6
Suppressed to Protect

My parents got divorced when I was eleven years old. It is very common when a family goes through a divorce for the children to blame themselves for the breakup. I was one of those kids and can recall feeling very sad, hurt and confused the day my parents shared their news. For me, this felt like the end of the world. I blamed myself and felt helpless. I couldn't make the sorrow I was feeling go away, and I couldn't stop it. I had no control over what was happening. As an adult I now understand that it wasn't my fault and I needed to experience that pain as part of my journey. My mother went through a long and deep depression and it was traumatizing to see her that way. I didn't want to be around it. I created a very negative label of the word *depression*, vowing that I would never allow myself to be *depressed*. I was overwhelmed with emotions that felt far bigger than me, so my defense mechanism switched those feelings off in order to protect myself. I became *numb*. From that point on, I really didn't acknowledge much about my feelings, and the only tool I developed for dealing with them was to stuff them down.

Whenever I was asked to think back to my earliest upset in life, the first memory that would surface would be my parents' divorce. But after digging deeper in therapy, I still felt like something was unresolved, that there was definitely an earlier "upset." Well, during my three year struggle, through lots of therapy, I came to uncover and remember a few devastating and disempowering incidents that adversely affected my self-confidence. The first disturbing memories that came to light had to do with my being bullied in school at the age of eight. At recess one afternoon after the bell rang for us to return to class, I was attacked by two peers who I thought were my friends.. The two boys cornered me by a tree and wouldn't let me return to school. I felt so picked on and small. I couldn't understand why they were being so mean to me. That same day after school, they hid in some bushes that I had to walk through to get home, and proceeded to jump on my back, sit on me and shove my face into the dirt, telling me to, "Eat your dinner!" Someone intervened after what felt like forever, and told them to leave me alone. I cried myself home and buried the incident deep inside like I had done with other upsets many times before.

I remembered an even earlier and more crushing trauma that occurred before the incident in the bushes. I had been molested when I was five years old by a neighborhood boy. For some reason he was the only choice one evening for a babysitter, so my mom hired him to come over. I was very shy, so my brother did most of the talking in the beginning. The boy talked with us on the couch for a while, then asked us if we wanted to play hide and seek. He would jump out and scare me when he was hiding. I remember feeling uneasy the whole evening. He had us get ready for bed, and after I'd been relaxing for a bit, about to doze off and my brother was asleep, he came into my room "to check on me" and asked if he could "keep me company." He lay down next to me and started telling me how my brother was a bad boy and I was a good girl. He worked very hard to earn my trust in a very short time.

Unfortunately, I was a very shy little girl and didn't have my voice yet. Therefore, I was an easy target. I did as he asked, and the next thing

I knew he was on top of me and I was stuck. I couldn't move and was very scared. He told me to keep quiet and stay still. He scared me, so I did what he said. I remember his collar hitting me in my face and the smell of him being quite repulsive. I wanted him to stop and get off me. Whenever I would squirm he would tell me to stay still, and I was very scared of him so I listened. I wanted my brother to come save me. He was just on the other side of the wall, yet I couldn't scream. My brother and I were big fans of super heroes. I attempted to arouse my own super powers in the moment. I remember trying to *think* to my brother that I needed help. I strained so hard trying to reach him. I pictured him running to my room any second, but he didn't show up.

I must have deeply repressed the memory of exactly what took place when he was attacking me and forcing himself on me, but I don't think it went the way the neighborhood boy had hoped. I recall him jumping up off of me and having a complete mood change, becoming suddenly angry. His kind disposition took a sharp turn into panic and he became threatening. He said horrible things to me to make me feel like my parents wouldn't love me if I told them what had just transpired. He begged me over and over again to promise I wouldn't talk to them and told me that bad things would happen if I did. When he finally left my room, I was in shock. I wanted my mommy and daddy so badly. I wanted to tell them what happened, but the boy's words about my parents not loving me anymore and not believing me if I told them what occurred kept repeating in my mind. The intensity of that trauma caused so much helplessness and shame that I couldn't process it rationally, and ended up crying myself to sleep.

I can remember going into my mom's room the following morning wanting desperately to tell her what had happened. I wanted her to drag it out of me and relieve me of the horrible nightmare. Again, I tried to get her to read my mind like I had wished my brother could, but nothing happened. I walked out of her room with overwhelming guilt, shame and sorrow that I couldn't understand or handle on my own, so my mind hid the incident away for forty years.

Now, as I write these words, having to remember and relive the incident, I realized that was the moment when I lost my voice and my faith in myself. My world shifted and I no longer trusted my wings to carry me. From that moment on, it was difficult for me to share my viewpoint with others because I felt I'd be judged and disliked. That very disturbed young man's words, on the night he babysat for me, had a debilitating impact on my life. The way I saw myself and how I thought people saw me was negatively skewed from that day on. I thought I had to like what others liked and agree with others' perspectives in order to be accepted in any circle or in any relationship. I didn't know my own worth. I didn't know that I could be loved for who I was and for what I believed. Thankfully, after much soul searching, I now know my worth.

When I look back at my first intimate experiences as a young lady, I remember feeling blocked and inhibited, shameful, dirty and bad. I couldn't understand where those feelings were coming from. My husband even noticed my inhibitions. Years into our marriage, he confided that he felt like something traumatizing must have happened to me based on the way I first expressed myself with him during our intimate moments. After uncovering the incident with the neighbor boy, I now understand why I had also found myself in dreadful predicaments of date rape a few times in high school and college. During those traumas, I was once again unable to find my voice, which caused me to feel disappointed and angry at myself. I couldn't understand why I allowed myself to get into those situations. I became even more upset when I didn't have the confidence or courage to stand up for myself.

I can't help but think of the millions of other innocent young ladies who have also found themselves in such devastating and violating situations. If anything like that has ever happened to you and you haven't shared your story with anyone yet, please reach out and get the assistance you deserve to heal your wounds. No matter how much shame or insecurity you may feel about what you experienced, know that you are stronger and more courageous than you realize. You are more than enough. Speak up and free yourself of your nightmare. It is your birthright to be happy. It is so important to teach our children self-confidence, self-worth and self-love. We must make it crystal clear that they have every right to use their voices, express their beliefs and be their most authentic selves. If only I had learned and developed such self-esteem in my younger years, I could have saved myself decades of sorrow.

••

"It's not about finding your voice, it's about giving yourself permission to use your voice." ~Kriss Carr

••

GOD'S LOVE

God's love is questioned by many, not knowing if it's true.
For many things are good in life, and others very cruel.

We want to believe our God is powerful… loving, guiding and fair,
Then devastating things happen to lots of good people and
it appears our God doesn't care.

Why believe in a Higher Power that hurts us and doesn't
make things right?
Then leaves us hopeless, sad and confused, not knowing
how to continue the fight.

Instead of blaming God when things get really bad,
Embrace God's love, courage and strength, to help you feel glad.

God's love is pure and real… it's everywhere all the time.
If you listen closely you'll hear God's love in the sound of a
cheery wind chime.

Just look at the beauty all around, like a rainbow in the sky.
God's love is even in our favorite foods, like a delicious
apple pie.

So look around and you will see God's love in your family
and friends.
And always know, no matter what you're going through,
God's love for you never ends.

SCENE 7
Searching for Higher

A fter the Thanksgiving situation, I found a new doctor and again had confidence that she would help get me the solace I so desperately craved. Despite how opposed I was to medications, I was so miserable that I was willing to give anything a chance. The new doctor put me on two medications, Xanax and Zoloft, and again, we waited. Would this pharmaceutical cocktail finally rescue me? I hadn't slept well for six months, my symptoms were wearing on me, and I had lost twenty pounds. While I once thought that I could stand to lose a few pounds, this was no way to lose them. Plus, I really couldn't enjoy the benefits of my new hot bod in the heat of the agony I was feeling. What a reminder to be careful about what we wish for and how we wish for it to manifest! I learned that if I want something, I have to be very specific in my vision.

After a month on the meds, and not being able to figure out the proper dosage or the right time to take them, I realized I was spinning further out of control. The medication was causing even worse anxiety and bringing about terrible thoughts. I became extremely frightened and even more desperate for help than I had been before. I remember riding in the car with my sister-in-law, hysterically crying and begging her to help me find relief. I imagined there had to be an inpatient holistic healing center that could take care of me. I was having such a challenging time holding on anymore. I didn't want to burden my family and friends any longer. I strongly believed that everything had to be happening for a reason, so I just continued praying that it would all be over soon. Unfortunately, though, the days continued to come and go with no answers, no relief, and ever-increasing worry and concern.

I was never a very religious person, but I always believed in some kind of Higher Power, and had a sense of spirituality. My health crisis definitely had me searching more for God and answers. I couldn't understand why God would put me through what I went through for nothing. In the pain, though, I finally gained an awareness of my own relationship with myself. Before then, I had never been forced to acknowledge my past hurts or to deal in any healthy way with my disappointments. I had never taken full ownership of my life or my place in the world. My trauma was telling me that it was time to step it up. I got that message right away, after I fell, and I continued to pay attention and to listen for signs and opportunities to grow.

I started working with a therapist, listening to amazingly inspirational speakers online, and finally began to recognize my own relationship with myself and others. I had been such a good faker my whole life, acting as if things were always great in my world. I never wanted to burden anyone with my pain, so I kept it all to myself. I clearly had work to do. Talk about major explosions that needed to happen to shake me up. If only I knew what I was creating for myself by suppressing my pain all those years, I may have rethought my choices.

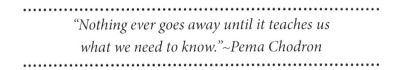

"Nothing ever goes away until it teaches us
what we need to know."~Pema Chodron

SCENE 8
Imprisoned in My Own Skin

By the end of December 2014, after taking Xanax all month, I spiraled down an even darker hole. I was having unsettling, disturbing thoughts and I felt totally detached from myself, like I was floating in another realm (but not detached enough *not* to feel my pain). I felt extremely frightened for my well being. I was so desperate for relief, sleep and any modicum of comfort. During that time, I was taken to the ER for the third time in two months. I waited for more than *six hours* for a doctor to come in and assess my situation. By the time a doctor got to me, it had been at least eight hours since I had taken my last Xanax. Surprisingly, I noticed my head clearing up, and an awareness of *me* starting to return. It was quite a relief in the sense that I started to feel more like myself again. My symptoms were still peaking - I was still a prisoner in my own body - but at least I was not also imprisoned by the terrifying effects of Xanax. Amen! It became clear to me during that ER visit that I would never again touch Xanax. As intense as my anxiety still was, after living with it for a while, I finally realized that anxiety alone wouldn't kill me. I chose to just breathe through it as I waited for the doctor to return. And from here forward, I realized that I would be in a better place even living with anxiety than I would be trying to live with the effects Xanax had on me. Xanax was FIRED!

During that trip to the ER, a social worker came in to visit me. We had a long chat about my situation, and discussed the best way to move forward in order to get me well again. She suggested that I stay in their inpatient program. My very first thoughts were, "Oh *hell* no! I just need sleep! I am fine! I am not going to stay in a looney bin!" Boy, did I have some growing up to do! Again, I was so concerned about what others would think of me, that I put their imagined judgment ahead of my own needs. I stubbornly went home that night... then checked myself into the program the next day. "Looney Bin," here I come!

Holy crap, I was so nervous to leave my family and check into a place where I would be on lockdown. At this point in the game, my biggest priority was sleep. I didn't even know how bad things were underneath it all, I just knew that I needed SLEEP! My room consisted of three cold walls of concrete, a small sink, and a toilet. It was the closest I'd ever been to a jail cell, from what I'd seen on TV and from my visit to Alcatraz, anyway. The door had to remain open at all times as a safety precaution. I hated it already, but I was hoping the doctors would find a cocktail that would knock me out so that I could just sleep for a few days... and then I'd wake up from this nightmare.

Every evening, the inpatients lined up to get their meds for the night. It was so surreal that I was one of them - like a prisoner waiting in line for her serving of flavorless mush on a tray. The first night I arrived, I was put on a new sleep medication. I was actually excited to be starting on the new meds, hoping that I would finally be able sleep. So much for that dream. On the first night, I only slept for three hours, then spent the rest of the night tossing and turning. A staff member checked on all patients every thirty minutes or so, and the light from the hallway was constantly beaming on my face, in my eyes. This was no place to get any sleep.

During the day, it was recommended that all patients participate in group discussions and lessons. I was committed to giving this place my very best, so I showed up to those meetings - unrested, groggy, extra anxious, feeling like crap, and just praying that I would find the relief I needed. At the beginning of each class, we filled out a survey about our current well-being, then shared it out loud. "I'm not suicidal, I don't hate myself or my life, I merely want to sleep," was how many of my well-being surveys went. I truly believed, at the time, that sleep would literally cure me. It had been so long since I had experienced a deep and solid sleep. My body felt permanently switched on with massive cortisol and adrenaline, and nothing I tried would shut it off. I would feel sporadic, crazy zapping sensations through my limbs, and my brain always felt like it was rocking, with moments of intense pressure that I cannot even put into words. I was miserable.

The days were very long sitting inside that depressing room, so I did my best to find any amount of contentment or even distraction. When I could find the energy, I would do yoga poses or squats in the small hallway that joined our rooms. I became friendly with a few of the nice ladies in my unit. They really helped me understand and change my viewpoint about these facilities. My fellow inpatients were just "regular people" who were suffering from different situations, and needed support. There was nothing strange or different about them. I wasn't any better of a person than they were. We were all suffering from different intense circumstances that most people couldn't even fathom.

My heart went out to my fellow unit mates, and I prayed for their relief and their speedy return to their own special lives. It was very hard for all of us to put our lives on hold, and to step out of our familiar environments to get the help we so desperately needed. While it was a relief to hear that my family was surviving just fine without me around, it also brought about feelings of separation and loneliness. As a mother of three young kids, I especially yearned to be back with them, participating in all of their activities, and being the healthy, functional, supportive mother they needed. It broke my heart to think that I would never get back that precious time with them. I had so much anger inside of me. If there was a God, (which I always believed there was), then why the hell was He letting this happen to me?

I couldn't comprehend why my painful situation was lasting so long. I was urgently looking for help from too many people and places, and not getting the relief I needed. My time at this inpatient program was no different. I spent my days at the hospital writing in my journal, trying my best to be positive and to be a good sport. After a couple of days of intense anxiety, my body couldn't take it anymore, so I surrendered and asked for a medication that I had not tried before. Another random drug cocktail for me, please. Then, I went to lie down to see if I could take a nap and finally drift off for a bit. I got in a few minutes of dosing before the shit really hit the fan. I jumped up in the biggest panic I had experienced yet. My brain was beyond scrambled and my heart was pounding. I ran into the hall and fell to the ground, screaming for help. The reaction I was having from this med felt like I was bouncing down a San Francisco hill in a huge tire, and I was completely helpless. It was terrifying. I just wanted my husband to hold me. I wanted to go home.

At that facility, they were throwing different drugs at me, and I still wasn't getting any sleep. From the cold floor of the depressing hallway, I knew for certain that the program was not the place or answer for me. At first, a couple of the other patients came over to me, followed by staff members. They carried me back to my bed and asked if they could give me something sedating. I was so scared. I didn't feel safe putting more drugs in me. If I didn't settle down fast, however, I was sure that they would force some down my throat. Back in my sterile bed, I made a concerted effort to compose myself, even though the crazy sensations were still rattling my brain. I told everyone that I would be fine, and they all left the room except for one staff member. She sat and talked with me, instructing me to breathe and repeat a positive statement in my head. Imagine telling a tantruming two year old to just "calm down and breathe." It felt so condescending and ridiculous considering the state I was in. At that point, I was in pain, irritated and annoyed. I just wanted her to go away... I wanted it all to go away.

I called my mom on the fourth morning, very early, and begged her to come get me. I remember saying, "You are my mom, and I need you to listen to me and trust me. I need your help! Please come get me. This isn't working!" I don't think I have ever been so desperate in my life. Coincidently, later that morning, my doctor came in to discuss his findings with me, and informed me that there really wasn't anything they could do for me there. He suggested that I visit a sleep clinic. While I was excited to get the hell out of there and go home, I felt discouraged that I didn't get what I went there for. It all felt like a huge waste of time, and I was leaving there more sleep deprived than when I had arrived.

Because I wasn't well rested and I didn't want my kids to see me in so much agony, my mom and stepdad offered to have me stay with them for a while. Their home was a peaceful and quiet environment. They had lots of little shiny knick-knacks throughout the house that would catch my attention as I lay in distress on their couch. My mom collected cat and heart trinkets and always had flowers around, so there was plenty for my eyes to gaze at as I lay in misery. My mom would do her best to stay upbeat and distract me with card games and meaningful chats. My stepdad would listen to music with me, hoping it would be a good distraction. We listened to oldies like Jim Crose, which I really enjoyed. Music filled my soul with hope and love. Unfortunately, I still felt like my brain was being squeezed like a sponge and my limbs were sizzling like a bug on an electric bug zapper, so I could not fully enjoy those hopeful and loving vibes.

I would sit at the dinner table with my parents and do my very best to hold myself together. I was miserable but I didn't want to be "too much" for them to handle. No matter where I went, or who I was with, my throbbing head and fragile body came along. My home, with my immediate family, was the only place I could really have the breakdowns I so desperately needed to let out. I recall going for a walk with my mom in their neighborhood. My body was so frail and weak that I felt like the slugs were passing us by. We weren't very far from the house, but in my situation it felt like miles. At one point, I remember feeling extremely light headed and my vision blacking out. I had tons of anxiety blasting through me and I honestly thought I might die in that moment. I was scared to express the extent of my pain to my mom, but I could not move on my own. My mom had to hold me up and it took every ounce of energy I could muster to make it back to her house. As scary as that must have been for my mom, she really handled it well.

I think my loved ones acted strong in front of me, then had their own breakdowns when I wasn't around. I know that it was extremely hard for my mom to watch me go through what I did. She was confused and felt helpless like the rest of my family felt. It certainly brought us closer, though. During our time together, I was able to express my childhood upsets and disappointments that I experienced with her, which I had stuffed away in order to remain her "good girl," and not upset her. My mom was very compassionate in response, and it felt so good to be seen, heard and understood by her. I no longer felt resentment or disappointment towards my mom. I saw her as a beautiful, caring and compassionate soul who brings so much love and laughter to our family. She has worked through her own life struggles and I will always admire her strength and courage. I suppose that is where I got mine.

> *"When things do not go your way,*
> *remember that every challenge - every*
> *adversity - contains within it the seeds for*
> *opportunity and growth."* ~Roy T. Bennett

SCENE 9
Dr. Smooth

"Saint Kelly" took time off work to fly with me out of town to see a neurologist with whom we were lucky enough to get an appointment. He was very well known for his work. People came from all over the world to see him. Again, I was hoping that he would be my saving grace, and that with his expert guidance, I could put the crisis behind me. Getting through the airport was extremely unpleasant for me as it was difficult for me to stand upright in conjunction with the hypersensitivity of all my senses. I pushed through, hoping that it would be the last time I had to experience such discomfort. I prayed that I was at the finish line. I listened to music on the plane, which helped me get into my zone, so that I didn't break down in front of people. The brain damage that I had sustained definitely had a huge effect on my emotional well-being, and coupled with the extreme lack of sleep - I was usually a wreck. I felt like a jack-o-lantern with a knife plunged through my head, which I could not remove no matter what I tried. I couldn't help but just sob from the pain, no matter where I was. Usually, it was at a doctor's office with plenty of people around, and let me tell you, breaking down in public was a great way to wash my inhibitions away and stop caring about what others thought. I was so vulnerable and raw in the state I was in, I really couldn't care how I was perceived. In fact, in an interesting way, my pain made me feel closer to everyone.

I just loved everyone. I felt so genuine and real. I came to understand the importance of connection along this life journey. I just wanted connection, and to let others know their importance, no matter what their life circumstance. I was connecting with the true me, the dichotomy was beautiful and devastating all at once. I was on the nauseating spinny-ride at a carnival and I had no idea when it would end, but at least I was having profound realizations. I realized that helping others feel connected was part of my purpose.

We waited in a dark room for the doc to come see me. I cried, as usual, from lack of sleep and lack of ability to control anything about my situation. When the doctor finally came into the room to see me, it was a welcomed entrance. I immediately felt comfortable in his presence. It didn't hurt that he had a deep, soft, silky-smooth, alluring voice that caught both my and Kelly's attention and put us into a sweet trance. He proceeded to spend an hour running tests on me, which were no fun at all. He put certain glasses over my eyes called photophobia lenses, so that he could track my eye motions on his screen. I had to follow dots, colors and shapes. It took a lot of energy for me to focus on the tasks I was being given, which had to be done correctly, or else I had to start all over. I felt like a rat in a maze. One test he conducted involved having me sit in a chair and spin very fast. I had to keep my eyes wide open so he could see how they reacted to the spinning. I felt dizzy enough as it was without being spun like a dreidel, so the whirling only made things worse. I was committed to staying in my zone, though, because I wanted to get answers. When it was finally time for the doctor's prognosis, he gave us a very long explanation, with lots of code language, which was all Greek to me. I paid attention as best I could, hopeful that he was my savior, at last. I was also mesmerized by his voice, which made listening to his jargon more bearable.

Back at the hotel room, Kelly and I had a good laugh about our shared impression of Dr. Smooth. A good laugh was always appreciated in my situation. One of the wonderful things about Kelly, besides her being so very patient, tolerant and compassionate towards me, was that she was truly invested in my recovery. She would get so excited when she felt we were getting answers. We would do our own mini celebration dance in hopes of results. We did a celebratory dance even though it turned out that there was nothing to celebrate. I was sent home with just some exercises from the doctor, and told to return once I got my sleep under control. Lacking sleep impeded any accurate results. I was also on two medications that didn't seem to be helping, and they were interfering with his ability to properly diagnose me. I pushed through the airport and flight once again and made my way home - back to sleepless nights, agonizing days, and nothing to do but dwell on my horrible situation. I was almost a year in at that point, and I wasn't seeing any light in the tunnel, not even a tiny speck. I chose to put my faith in the wise words of Wayne Dyer, "You will see it when you believe it." I still needed to wrap my head around "feeling" something before it showed up. Just because I couldn't see the light in the tunnel didn't mean it wasn't there... somewhere.

•••
"Every time you are able to find some humor in
a difficult situation, you win." ~Unknown
•••

SCENE 10
Searching for Signs

One of my favorite books that I read during my dark days was "The Universe Has Your Back" by Gabrielle Bernstein. Being open, raw and vulnerable from lack of sleep, my throbbing head and my desperation for a helping hand, I would pay close attention to "inspirational junkies" who would cross my path in the form of a mentor, a book or a podcast. I was especially fascinated by Gabrielle's explanation of the type of communication we have with The Universe. She spoke a lot about looking for signs that can guide us along our paths. I had experienced moments in my life when it felt like I was receiving a sign, but would then wave it off as a coincidence. Looking back, I now understand that those signs were real. One of my favorite memories of when I asked for a sign from The Universe was when I was pregnant with my daughter. I had manifested at a young age that "when I grew up" I would have two boys and a girl, in that order. Well, I had my two sons at that point and was carrying my third child. My soul already knew she was a girl but my ego didn't want me to get too excited, so it created much uncertainty for me to ponder.

My family and I were on a vacation and I was taking a walk along a magnificent beach. I asked for a sign from above to reveal the sex of my unborn child. Right then, I looked down at a piece of seaweed that was in the shape of a capital "G," which clarified that my baby was a girl. I was then guided to look up at a mountain that had a large, white "K" mounted on it. The only name for a girl that my husband and I agreed upon at that time was Kennedy. In that moment, I felt a deep understanding and truth that was a hundred percent aligned with The Universe. Sadly, that knowing sense I felt did not last long, as I had not yet learned to trust myself or the signs from above. I allowed doubt to creep in. I'd tell myself, "You had better not get too attached to having a daughter, as you wouldn't want your possible son to feel unwanted." I came to acknowledge my connection to source when my daughter was born. Clearly, my question that day on the beach had been accurately answered.

Another time that I received a clear sign from The Universe was when I asked for a sign regarding my marriage. While my soul had guided me to my husband and knew that he and I were meant to walk life's path together, I would often question whether he and I were truly meant for each other. While I am very grateful to have been raised in a comfortable lifestyle, it was easy for me at that young age to get caught up in evaluating my self-worth compared to my observation of my peers. I brought my insecurities into my marriage and would sometimes question my relationship when my husband and I would get into an argument or when he didn't live up to the standards I felt I deserved. Our arguments were usually about me not feeling a connection that I desired or about something to do with money, gifts, holidays or home repairs. There were also so many wonderful things I loved about my husband. For one, he was born with a giving heart and would be the first to step up and help a friend or family member with any favor. He was loyal, compassionate, funny and I loved laughing with him. I never doubted his love for me, even when he didn't show it in the way I wanted.

One day, halfway through my three-year nightmare, I was walking around my backyard with that same gnawing concern about my marriage, which now had seventeen years to build. Being in immense physical pain only heightened any of my previously unresolved issues. After listening to many spiritual leaders profess that physical ailments were a direct reflection of emotional wounds, I wondered if all my pain was actually The Universe telling me that I shouldn't be in my "imperfect" marriage any longer. I was willing to part ways with my husband if it meant that I would receive the relief I urgently craved. As my bare feet glided across the grass, I told The Universe, "Show me a four-leaf clover if I should tell Doron I want to split up." I immediately looked down and there it was, crystal clear, dew-glistening before my eyes. I couldn't believe it. This time, I chose to trust that the four-leaf clover was a sign from The Universe to have that conversation with my husband.

With my symptoms running wild, I felt a sense of confidence that I was on the right path towards healing by ending my marriage. The day I found the four-leaf clover, my kids must have been with their aunts and cousins. I wondered if they would hate me or if they would be negatively affected the same way I was when my parents divorced. I decided that no matter what, I would stay committed to the sign. When my husband walked in that evening, I immediately had him sit down and talk with me. I was very nervous that he would get extremely angry, defensive and mean. The exact opposite happened. He was clearly caught off guard and took some deep breaths to take it all in. We discussed my request for a while and then he said he wanted to go meet up with his brother for some support. When he returned, he told me that he was going to stand by me until I was completely healed (as there wasn't anyone else to watch over me the way he knew he could), and if I still felt the same way after getting back on my feet, we could split up and would remain friends and co-parents. WOW!

I didn't see that coming but I sure was amazed by his generosity, his love for me, and his commitment to my well-being.

As it turned out, I wasn't aware of exactly why The Universe gave me the message, through that four-leaf clover, to have that painful conversation with my husband. I now realize that I was being instructed to broach the subject of divorce with my husband, in order to see his authentic love for and commitment to me. His unconditional support, even in the face of such a blow to his heart, meant so much more to me than flowers, jewelry or name-brand clothing ever could. He loved me for me, and was going to be sure I was back on my feet before ever leaving my side. We still had much to accomplish in order to work more cohesively as a couple. After his proclamation to stand by me, we chose to work even harder towards a more satisfying relationship. Our connection has been more rewarding than I could ever have imagined. I will be forever grateful for that sign from The Universe telling me to have that conversation with my husband. That heart-to-heart brought us closer than we had ever been before, and enabled us to focus on what we love about each other. We were then able to truly enjoy each other's company and have come to cherish the times we are blessed to dance, play and explore all of the gifts of life together.

....

"You won't miss a sign from The Universe.
It will keep getting louder and louder
until you get it." ~Anonymous

....

SCENE 11
Accepting Therapy

When my parents got divorced, they wanted my brother to talk to a therapist about his feelings, mostly because he was acting out. I, however, was not acting out; I was the quiet one. I do recall being asked if I wanted to see the therapist as well, and I quickly refused. Back then I thought that going to a therapist meant there was something mentally wrong with me, which meant that I wasn't a "cool'" kid. And being the easy-going, agreeable, "I've got it all together" gal, there was no way in hell I was going to see a therapist and ruin my self image. So, I continued to shove down my feelings like the stuffing in a teddy bear. I clamped on my armor so that it would forever protect me… or so I thought. Life eventually took its course, and my armor stopped protecting me from myself. When I went away to college in Arizona, my insecurities rose to a boil, and I began experiencing uncontrollable bursts of crying. I recall one day when I called my mom and told her, "I will do anything now, even see a therapist. I need help!" When I returned home from college that summer, I started seeing my first therapist. With her, I finally started to dive into my issues.

Therapy, along with all the discoveries I made as a result of my "wake up fall," woke me up to a whole new perspective on many conditions with which I was struggling. These included depression, anxiety and many other aspects of myself that I had been afraid to look at in the past. Through my experience, I learned to accept myself in whatever state I was in, at any given moment - even if I felt vulnerable, raw or broken (feelings which I previously felt too ashamed to let surface). Acceptance is the first step towards healing. I worked with a few other therapists in my adult life who helped me understand the importance of accepting ourselves right where we are. About five months after my fall, when things had become extremely challenging for my family and me (little did we know what a terribly long haul we had to go), I was guided to the *perfect* therapist for me at that time. Susan was one of the most supportive, compassionate and kind-hearted people I had ever met. The child in me was still fragile like a porcelain doll, and Susan was the perfect person to help nurture and comfort my inner child. Her office was set up with calming colors and unique decorations. I would lie down on the couch as soon as I entered the room and get myself as comfortable as possible, melting into the cushions. Meeting with Susan was my escape from my chaotic and painful environment. I felt safe in her space, and appreciated her calming voice and gentle smile. We had so many meaningful and helpful conversations, and of course lots of tears. I don't recall exactly why my sessions with Susan ended, but I will be forever grateful for the love and support she gave me.

A few months later, I was recommended to another wonderful therapist named Heidi. The Universe came through, yet again, and blessed me with a knowledgeable, deeply caring and understanding mentor with whom I felt very comfortable and safe. As usual, I would do my best to relax on her couch, while admiring her soothing decor and fashionable outfits. She was always well put together. My tears would pour forth, and she would comfort me with her warmth and sincerity. Heidi always had the best advice, and her words gave me hope for a bright future. My perspective on therapy has shifted dramatically over the years. Some people try so hard not to be vulnerable, that they won't ask for help when they need it. They strive to appear like they can handle everything just fine on their own. I understand these people well, as I used to be "these people." I spent too much of my life with that "I don't need help, I can handle it myself" attitude, and it didn't improve anything in my life for the better. I sabotaged myself with that detrimental stance about therapy. I have come to understand that humans are not meant to contend with life's struggles alone. Part of our growth comes from the connections we experience with one another during both joyful and trying times. There are many insightful people whose purpose is to serve others as therapists, and instead of judging them, we can have gratitude for therapists, and for their wise counsel when we need it most. There is something very special about a therapist-patient relationship, especially when you find the right fit. I can't recommend having the experience of talk therapy highly enough. It certainly transformed my life.

••
"Having a need and needing help is not
a sign that you're weak, it's a sign that
you're human." ~Kate Northrup
••

I AM

I am my breath as it flows in and out.
I am my heartbeat that beats without a doubt.
I am my blood and organs too.
I am my whole body that knows just what to do.
I am an intelligence we cannot see.
I am the bigger part of me.

SCENE 12
Hope for Healing

By April 2015, I was seven months in, and feeling like I had reached my tolerance threshold. Trying to convince myself of the old adage, "God never gives us anything we can't handle," was *not* working. I felt no relief, found no answers about my mystery condition, and had no good ideas about how to heal it. Everyone around me was getting antsy and feeling more and more helpless. I was searching high and low for something to help me heal. I remembered my kids' awesome Hebrew teacher, Abby, talking to me about a magical, healing oasis called Hippocrates Health Institute (HHI) in West Palm Beach, Florida. She was studying there at that time for her Health Educator/Coaching Certification and really believed their protocol would be transformational for me. Nothing seemed to be working at home, and I was starting to feel like I needed a new environment, so the idea of rejuvenating at a healing retreat center in a tropical location certainly appealed to me.

I found myself feeling torn. On the one hand, I loved my family and felt as though I needed their support. On the other hand, it was agonizing to endure my physical, mental and emotional pain, then just sit around each day and watch my family live their lives. I can't say I wasn't experiencing some jealousy watching them live their "normal, comfortable" lives, either. I desperately wanted to go to Hippocrates, but I wasn't sure if I could even physically make the trip.

Abby gave me the number of an intuitive life coach named Dawn who she had met in Florida during her time there, and I decided to give her a call. I immediately felt a soothing warmth and connection to Dawn, which brought me hope. After speaking with her and getting some intuitive guidance, I decided to give Hippocrates a try. I set up a few in-person appointments with Dawn, too, for the time that I would be in her area.

I booked the stay at HHI for their three-week Life Transformation Program, but I was in no shape to travel on my own. I couldn't handle any kind of light besides daylight, so trying to get through the airport with all of its horrible lighting would create massive discomfort and anxiety on top of what I already had going on. Scents were also a major trigger, so being around perfumes and colognes really set me off. I called my dear friend, Heather, who had been my best friend since high school, and I practically begged her to accompany me to the healing retreat center. Bless her heart, Heather rearranged her schedule so that she could assist me in getting to HHI and spend five nights there with me to help me get acquainted with the grounds and the program.

As we walked into the airport, Hippocrates-bound, bright and early, I had to cover my eyes with an eye mask within the first couple of minutes, as I began to feel that all-too-familiar buzzy and irritating sensation from the lights. I held on to Heather, as she led me through the airport, politely moving people out of our way. We chuckled about it, but under my eye mask, I could not help but ponder that this was what it must be like for blind people to make their way through the world. I felt utterly helpless. I wanted to see the people around us. I wanted to see color. It was dark and isolating in my dependent world behind my mask. And then, remembering the sage teachings of one of my recently discovered mentors, I surrendered. I recognized that airport experience as a lesson to trust Heather and the process and to accept what was currently happening. As soon as I did, my attitude shifted and a calm washed over me. We made it onto the airplane with relative ease. I had my eyes covered during our entire time in the airport. After takeoff, when the lights were dimmed, I removed my mask and felt grateful for my sight - acutely aware of one of the blessings in my life.

Heather was invaluable to me as a travel companion and as a guide at the Hippocrates Health Institute. My dear friend accompanied me around the property and helped me set up my weekly schedule, which she also took part in for the five days that she stayed there with me. Hippocrates was a magical place, indeed. It was a tropical jungle oasis in the midst of the concrete jungle that is West Palm Beach. Everyone there, staff and guests alike, were friendly and helpful. The daily workshops I attended gave me much-needed insights about my life, relationships, forgiveness and so much more. Emotionally, I had finally found some relief, and was praying for a better *me* to blossom out of the experience. Physically, I was still suffering. Due to the insomnia I had been experiencing long before I arrived, I was taking some meds, one of which was for sleep. After meeting with the doctor at Hippocrates, I decided to wean off the sleep medication first. Being the all-or-nothing gal I was, I took a big leap and tried simply skipping the sleeping pill altogether one night. That didn't go well. I sat up in bed and cried with such defeat, as I hadn't slept well for so long, and there I was, still not able to fall asleep. I felt horrible and wondered if HHI was really going to be my saving grace. Heather comforted me, and convinced me to take the meds for the night, then consult with the doctor in the morning. With the doctor's guidance and support, I ended up lowering my dosage by one milligram each night, until I had completely weaned myself off of the sleep medication. Now that was rewarding! I was able to sleep better, too, without the drugs.

One of HHI's main healing protocols is to administer wheatgrass juice enemas twice a day. Without getting too graphic, Heather and I had some good laughs about our first experiences with this process. Let's just say it was a shitty, yet liberating experience. Two enemas, two green juices, lots of sprouts and vegetable-based dishes, in addition to the therapeutic procedures and classes, are all part of the Hippocrates daily protocol for healing all disease (which is just dis-ease). After five days on the Hippocrates diet, I think Heather was very excited to get home and eat a big steak. Waving goodbye to her, I felt some insecurities creeping in like a child being left alone at school for the first time, and reminded myself that I was an adult and I could handle this on my own. Actually, I was way overdue for some alone time, where I could really work on improving the most important relationship, the one with myself. Plus, there were plenty of loving souls who I knew I could count on at the institute.

As Eckhart Tolle teaches, "When you lose touch with inner stillness, you lose touch with yourself. When you lose touch with yourself, you lose yourself in the world." I had definitely experienced that in my life. I had just finished reading "Stillness Speaks" by Eckhart Tolle, and had begun practicing his profound teachings, hoping to get back in touch with myself and the world. I would lie under five palm trees located in a row, right outside my little casita, and I would imagine they were my immediate family standing strong and supporting me. Sprawling out in the grass, staring up at the beauty of those forces of nature, dancing in the wind, gave me hope and reminded me to trust in the process of life. I would practice "being in stillness" and getting outside of my own head and my own pain, by focusing on and connecting with nature. I found Eckhart Tolle's teaching to be true, "Your innermost sense of self, of who you are, is inseparable from stillness. This is the I AM that is deeper than name and form." My palm tree family helped me to understand that daily.

When my parents divorced, I convinced myself that I didn't need anyone and I could take care of myself. Oh, the mind of an eleven-year-old, so certain yet so inexperienced. My health challenge forced me to see that we humans do indeed need one another. No one is an island. We aren't designed to handle all of our struggles on our own. In fact, I strongly believe that we are all teachers for one another. The people in our lives are teaching us all the time, whether the experiences are uplifting or not. Our interactions are shaping our lives and helping us grow into better versions of ourselves. Doing the dance of life with other people helps us to evolve into the people we were meant to be. I'm grateful that I met many such dance partners along my journey in Florida.

My first meeting with one of my favorite mentors, Dawn, was very emotional. I knew that she was a life coach and an intuitive person, but I had never before experienced anything like the session I had with her. Dawn, it turned out, was a medium. She could hear from those who had passed on, as well as from our spirit guides. I was definitely skeptical, but I was also extremely desperate for some answers. As I lay on her couch, Dawn had me close my eyes and breathe deeply three times, before she started talking. I remember sobbing over the messages that she kept bringing forth from my loved ones who had crossed over. What my guides were telling me sure did sound legitimate, but a part of me continued to question the whole process. It was a really great session, whatever it was, and I looked forward to seeing Dawn again. If nothing else, she gave me some comfort and reassurance that I would be okay.

Dawn and I continued our intuitive coaching sessions, each one bringing me more hope than the last. Emotionally, I continued to grow, and to see life in new and more positive ways, though I could not understand why my symptoms weren't improving. It truly felt like the Universe had knocked me over; as if It had been yelling at me all along, and I had been ignoring It. Now, It had my full and uninterrupted attention. I was all ears! So, when I experienced the awesome moments of insight and discovery, I assumed that the improvement of my symptoms would follow… but they did not. Great expectations, great disappointments. I grew more disheartened as time went on, because I couldn't understand why I would be given so much awareness and growth, only to remain trapped in my disturbed body. I had so much excitement inside, and a zest for living like I had never felt before, but I was still physically stuck. It was extremely frustrating, though I felt grateful for the relationships I made during my time in Florida.

I forged a few close bonds with people during my first week at Hippocrates, but it wasn't until the second week that I met Jadzia. She was half my age, but we connected right away. I felt an instant and deep connection with her, and I quickly started to refer to her as *my niece*. We shared our stories with each other, had meals together and became very close. It was nice to have a friend who understood and supported me, and who I could be supportive of, as well. When Heather left, I had a room to myself for the next entire week. During that time, I started to feel more independent again, and I actually enjoyed the private time with myself. For the last week of the program, I ended up moving into Jadzia's room with her and two other ladies. It was fun having *roomies*, and it reminded me of summer camp. I was missing my family, but at the same time, I was scared to go back home to the environment in which I had been so miserable.

Even though I could still feel all of my uncomfortable sensations, and I knew that I still had a long way to go to feel well, I felt safe at HHI. I had plenty of time to myself, and I was forced to stop and take a look at certain parts of me that I had never investigated. Who was I? What were my likes and dislikes? What did I really want out of life? I was getting so much support from the other guests, workshop facilitators and from Dawn. I was in a place where I could truly focus on loving myself. It felt empowering and I wanted more. I came from a world where I was never encouraged to get to know myself or do any work on myself; a world where most people did whatever they could to appear "perfect" on the outside, as if they had no struggles, no worries, no concerns. They tended to judge those who did have obvious problems. As Wayne Dyer said, "When you judge another person, you don't define them. You define yourself as someone who needs to judge." A person has to be in a lot of pain or disconnected from their soul to live like that, judging others and pretending to be "perfect" all the time, feeling like they can't even be human or imperfect at all to be loved or accepted.

Thankfully, I found the exact opposite to be true of the people I met at HHI. I encountered people with all sorts of health issues and from every walk of life. Those people were real, authentic souls. It was refreshing and inspiring to be around down-to-earth, no-nonsense, tell-it-like-it-is people. Oh, and I'm not putting the lost-soul "pretenders" down… I was one! I'm just pointing out that it was freeing to be able to show my true colors and meet people who were vulnerable and trusting enough to show me theirs. At Hippocrates, I came to see that life is an incredible gift we are given. We ought not waste it trying to be something we are not.

I started getting used to my environment at Hippocrates: the jungle-like feeling of the grounds, the clean and healthy foods, the supremely kind people… it was a paradise. And as life would have it, just as I started settling in, my stay began drawing to a close. It was bittersweet. On the one hand, I really enjoyed what I was experiencing at the healing retreat center. On the other hand, I missed my family. I couldn't help but hope that upon my return home, I would continue to improve, and my health crisis would end swiftly. I wanted that so badly. Then, I could jump back into life, and my loved ones would no longer have to care for me or worry about me. I could drive my kids around and actually participate in life again. We could put this nightmare behind us. I remember feeling a lot of pressure to make that happen as my time at Hippocrates was drawing to a close.

I never was one for public speaking, but it was part of the protocol in order to graduate from Hippocrates' three-week Life Transformation Program. I wanted to believe that I was healed even though I still felt out of sorts. I had definitely come a long way from where I was when I arrived, so I was proud to share that. Jadzia filmed my "commencement speech," and encouraged me to post it on Facebook. I wasn't even on Facebook at that time, but I wanted an easy way to keep in touch with her so I joined. I felt a little uncomfortable posting such a personal video as most people didn't even know what I was going through. I also felt more pressure to heal, as I didn't want people to see me slip down the rabbit hole again after making so much progress at HHI and stating so in my speech. I was still worrying so much about how others perceived me. I clearly still had more soul searching to do. Three steps forward, one step back.

One of the most important lessons I learned at Hippocrates was that life will throw us lemons sometimes, but those sour struggles can also be times of self-discovery, growth and triumph. We may not always enjoy the challenging parts of our journey here, but the self-awareness that is born out of struggle makes the process worth it. We need to strive to make lemonade in this life, together.

••
"All that I seek is already within me." ~Louise L. Hay
••

SCENE 13
Pity Party Transformed

noticed my phone barely ringing during my time of need, and felt the outside world getting further and further away from me. I had an awareness of life's continuous movement, which did not care about my damaged brain. I often felt isolated, alone and sorry for myself, thus I yearned even more for human connection. As humans it can be very uncomfortable showing up for our loved ones in times of crisis. Many of us grapple with what exactly to say or do for the person struggling. The depressing vibe coming from the ailing person can also turn people off and push them away. And we each bring our own insecurities and life experiences to the table, as well.

While I knew a lot of people, and I had a good handful of close friends, they didn't exactly show up for me the way my programming had expected. I developed unspoken expectations of certain friends in my life. For starters, I wished for them to be by my side, comforting me and reassuring me that I'd be OK, like Bette Midler's character in the movie *Beaches*, who was unconditionally there for her best friend until her last breath. Only in hindsight did I realize that my expectations were totally unfair and unrealistic. First off, the hell I was experiencing wasn't something that my friends even fully knew about, nor anything they could ever possibly comprehend. How could they ever have been "the wind beneath my wings" if they didn't know how drastically I was falling? I also felt like I didn't want to burden anyone at first, so I didn't share the full extent of what I was going through. While my painful symphony rose to a debilitating crescendo, my reclusiveness and resentment also increased. I became fully embodied in my role as conductor of the pity party, feeling alone and devastated that "nobody cared about me." The narrator in my mind created a dramatic sob story about no one being by my side, and I was the victim. And, while my husband will help anyone in need, he isn't a big fan of asking for help, either. He always told everyone, "We're good." We were far from good. Although, my husband did think that I was just "F.I.N.E.: Fucked-up, Insecure, Neurotic and Emotional." Yep, we were so "fine" that we didn't reach out for help. Our radio silence may have given our friends the wrong idea, causing them to give us space: space that I never wanted.

Life just kept moving around me. People kept going on about their business, while I stayed stuck as a prisoner in my own body. The gaping silence between myself and some of my friends triggered deeply rooted beliefs I had about not being worthy enough for people to show up for me. I kept the extent of my struggle hidden for three long years, yet I unfairly expected others to show up. It felt like I had been abducted and I was so insignificant that no one noticed or cared. At times, I would get so resentful that I would visualize myself in a healthy state, consciously choosing *not* to show up for people when they were in crisis. Of course, I knew the best version of myself would never ignore a friend in need, but after being a people-pleaser for my entire life, it felt good to be the spiteful bitch for a moment, even if only in my imagination.

I eventually worked through my pity party and outgrew the old beliefs I once held about myself and others, which no longer served me. I evolved beyond my immature thought process and strove to understand the reality of the situation, which was that most of my friends did not know the severity of my condition; and if they did, they were entitled to respond in their own ways, without any expectations from me. And the truth was, I wasn't *always* alone.

There were four amazing women for whom I will always be eternally grateful: my dear friends Ana, Connie, Heather and my sister-in-law Yael who had the patience, empathy and time to be there for me during my most desperate days. Whether it was by comforting me during my anxiety-ridden meltdowns, letting me rant and cry, or just taking me for a walk, they each showed up for me in their own individual and compassionate ways. They all made me feel more seen and important than I had felt in a very long time.

I can recall lying in a hammock in Ana's backyard, a place where I found an inkling of peace, gazing at the trees above me and wishing I were as free as the flying birds. Ana and I would meet regularly for our "therapy" sessions, each of which would strengthen my soul for another day. I recall a time when Ana came to visit me and while we stood side-by-side in my driveway, about to part ways for the day, I confided in her that I didn't think I could go on much longer. Tears began to stream down her face as she said compassionately, "I need my friend here with me!" That moment was a wake-up call where I realized my worthiness from another's viewpoint.

Connie helped to show me my value as well, through her love and dependability. She would drive me to appointments, coach me in my breathing when I needed to calm down, and do her best to comfort me when I felt my world was ending. She picked me up one day when I was seriously struggling in the midst of one of my panic attacks, and brought me to her house. I lay outside on her deck while she called some of the health practitioners I was working with at the time to ask them for guidance about how to handle me. The time that Connie spent caring for me and her dedication to my recovery went above and beyond friendship.

Heather would routinely call to check up on me, and to let me know she was always there for me no matter what I needed from her. As a best friend since high school, I knew I could rely on her through thick and thin. She escorted me across the country to Hippocrates Health Institute, gave me her shoulder to cry on, and offered her encouraging brand of insight and wisdom, bringing me hope and strength during some of my darkest days. Her amazing husband, Steve, generously gifted me his skilled chiropractic services in hopes that he could help me find peace of mind.

My sister-in-law, Yael, spent countless hours comforting me over the phone, looking up treatments for my symptoms, taking me for drives and walks, and consoling me. I spent many days curled up in her bed just to be in her supportive company and in a different environment than my own. I feel so grateful to have had Yael on my side as both a family member and a friend. All four of those beautiful souls were not only there for me, they were also exceptionally caring and available for my kids. They would drive them to and from school, take them out for treats and check in with them regularly to see how they were coping.

I am also eternally grateful that I married into the tight-knit Kantor family that always has each other's backs, even in the toughest of times. My kids were so very blessed to have had additional adult role models - their grandparents, Bobba and Zeida, aunties and uncles - to console them, entertain them and love them through our three-year nightmare. Their loving cousins were also sources of light during such a dark time.

In retrospect, I wish that I had just reached out and called my friends when I wanted their support, instead of waiting for them to call and visit me, growing ever more resentful when the phone and doorbell didn't ring. Had I been radically honest with myself, told it like it was, stepped out of my comfort zone and asked for the help I needed, I believe that I would have received more of the unconditional love and support that I desired from more of my friends. My wish would be that we can all learn from my mistake. Don't hide your pain. Reach out to your loved ones and allow them to help you. Don't take the gift of serving away from them. And, no matter how uncomfortable it may be to show up for an ailing person, even if they don't reach out, we must step out of our comfort zones and show up anyway, however we can. Extending ourselves in service to others is a benevolent deed that will fill your heart beyond measure, and which will be deeply appreciated by the receiver.

••
*"Let others help you. You give honor to others
not only by taking care of them, but by allowing
them to take care of you."* ~Jocelyn Soriano
••

SCENE 14
Guiding Lights

People need each other. The idiom, "iron sharpens iron" comes from a real process, which highlights this concept. In Old Testament times, they would use one iron blade to sharpen another iron tool, which would make both tools more effective. As humans, we "iron blades" need others to help shave off the dull edges and sharpen our perspectives. Luckily, I found those character sharpeners who helped me to see the light when I needed guidance most (though I could not actually be in the light).

I had a horrible sensitivity to smells, sounds and light, so I could not look at screens. TV was out. Not only did I experience agonizing fight or flight sensations running through me at all times, but I couldn't even escape my constant discomfort with some mindless onscreen entertainment. If I ever even attempted to indulge in TV, the flashes of light from the screen would only amplify the tightness and pressure in my forehead, as if someone were squeezing my brain in a lemon press. I was never a huge TV fanatic, but I swore I would become a screen junky when this was all over. I would read uplifting books when my brain would allow. Sounds, however, were another story. What would have sounded like an innocuous family dinner to most, sounded to me like an ear-piercing screech as my kids' forks scraped against their plates, daily. I could hear the awful noises as if they were happening *right* next to me, though my kids were downstairs in the kitchen and I was all the way upstairs in my bedroom. I would cringe as if I'd heard nails on a chalkboard.

Since movies and reading were not viable options, I would listen to inspirational speakers online to help pass the time. The first mentor I discovered along my path to wellness was the brilliant and graceful Louise L. Hay. Her life story was quite fascinating, and her determination in healing her own health crisis ended up leading her down an insightful path as a healer, inspiring and motivating others to find their own way through their trauma. I would listen to her for hours at a time, trying to find the deeper spiritual meaning in my situation, carefully listening to each word she spoke for direction in healing myself. I was also given her inspirational quote cards that I would pick from weekly. I would hang them on my mirror and repeat the affirmations written on the cards throughout my long, drawn-out days. While it may not immediately appear that our words, thoughts and repeated affirmations are working for our greatest good, over time they definitely pay off and are worth every moment of our attention. Thank you, Louise, for all of your wisdom!

Another inspirational favorite of mine became Dr. Wayne Dyer, who is known as the "Godfather of the Self-Help Movement." He put his heart and soul into his work, teaching timeless wisdom to whomever would listen, and he was greatly admired and loved by his followers. His words would delicately flow from his lips with meaning and purpose. The lessons he taught really impacted my perspective on my life. He inspired me to keep pushing through my terrible situation, and whenever I felt completely derailed, I would find my way back onto my healing path with his gentle direction. I was completely transformed by his quote, "When you change the way you look at things, the things you look at change." It was a profound reminder to be more aware of how I perceive the world around me. Wayne inspired me deeply and gave me hope!

I also spent many hours listening to the teachings of Abraham Hicks. Abraham is a collective group of "Source Energy" spirits, who communicate through the body of the lovely Esther Hicks. Esther then translates Abraham's messages for her followers. "Abraham" was challenging for me. The information made so much sense and deeply resonated with me, yet I had an internal battle with skepticism, as I had never been introduced to anything quite like Esther and Abraham before in my very physically-focused world. Plus, when I would follow the suggestions to the best of my ability, I would not see any results. As Esther and Abraham teach, some things take longer to manifest than others, and my brain injury was clearly one of those things. I couldn't find my "downstream" flow in the amount of pain I was experiencing. Everything Esther relayed from Abraham seemed accurate to me, though. She never stumbled or said anything that would show any sign of her teachings not being legitimate, but I just had a hard time wrapping my head around such ethereal concepts. Nevertheless, I listened and listened and listened to pass the time, and my soul always felt connected to that wisdom. The information I was getting through Abraham, as well as from Louise and Wayne, was profound and emotionally transforming for me, even though I was not improving physically.

After spending so much time listening to those main mentors, I felt inspired to get out there and live it up, to find my purpose and focus primarily on loving myself and those around me. I felt a motivating excitement and urgency to be healed, and to begin living a more meaningful life, with all my newfound knowledge. The problem was, my brain wasn't healed yet, and I was beginning to wonder if it ever would be. No matter how many inspirational recordings I would listen to, and positive affirmations I would recite per day, nothing improved. No one could truly understand what I was up against. I looked "normal" on the outside, but there was a big problem within.

What was going on? No one, including the "experts," could figure it out. How was I going to live like this? What I was feeling was something that I could never see myself getting used to. I felt like I had a shock collar on, which was always set to a hundred percent. Could you get used to that? Could you go about your daily routine with that intensity charging through you? I decided I couldn't.

> *"Staying positive does not mean that things will turn out okay. Rather, it is knowing that YOU will be okay, no matter how things turn out."* ~Helen Barry

GRATEFUL

I am grateful for the rising sun and watching the squirrels having so much fun.

I am grateful for the beautiful trees and the changing colors of their autumn leaves.

I am grateful for the mountains so high and the sound of the birds as they fly on by.

I am grateful for the waves of the ocean, how the beauty of the beach brings me happy emotions.

I am grateful for the love of my life and dream about being his happy and healthy wife.

I am grateful for snuggling in his arms as I weep, his compassion and love are so very deep.

I am grateful for Sammy's strong, courageous style and the love I see in his warm, gentle smile.

I am grateful for Nathan's sweet, witty charm and the way that he hugs me squeezing tight with both arms.

I am grateful for Kennedy's humor, love and grace. The sound of her laughter and the big smile on her face.

I am grateful for the family and friends by my side, their love and support fill me up with much pride.

I am grateful for my body that I am getting to know, even if the healing process is so very slow.

I am grateful for the dreams and desires I see and I know there is a happy future for me.

SCENE 15
Two Steps Back

"Whenever I took a step forward, it seemed as though life was pushing me five steps back." ~Jenni Rivera

Returning home from HHI was exciting at first. I felt stronger than when I had left three weeks earlier, and I was so happy to see my family. My kids had been amazingly understanding and supportive during the entire time I was away. They were worried and sad for me, though thankfully they were very good at taking care of themselves. In my own childhood, during my parents' divorce, I felt left alone to deal with the pain of the situation. Not only were my parents struggling with their own situations, but my brother was also a bit of a handful at the time, acting out his upset. At least he was expressing himself and getting his feelings out. Therefore, my parents responsively focused on him. He was the squeaky wheel, and he got the *grease*. In my lack of understanding about effective communication, and having already suppressed my voice due to a previous childhood trauma, I took a more self-damaging approach. I felt like I didn't want to be a burden to my parents, so I stuffed my feelings down. I wish I had imitated my brother with his emotional outbursts like I copied him in so many other ways, as little sisters do. Then I would have made my feelings known and I would have received the comfort that I so desperately needed… but then there would be no overcoming trauma story here, and I would not have had to dig so deeply to find my purpose. I believe that the old saying is true, everything happens for a reason.

My kids, unlike me at their age, have a genuinely strong sense of self, surely because they have loving parents and a loving, supportive extended family, who they can count on no matter what. I will always be grateful for the whole family package I gained when I married my husband. With the strong Kantor foundation, my kids were able to adapt to our family's trying reality with grace. They showed up for me in so many special ways, one being playing games with me because I couldn't read books or watch TV. It was bad enough to be so miserably uncomfortable day after day, but it was also irritating not to be able to do anything to distract myself from the hell I was experiencing (or should I say *entertain* myself; nothing could *distract* me from what was happening). Daytime talk shows are painful to watch, but I would have even taken that sensationalized drama over what I was experiencing. Playing games came closer to distracting me from myself than anything else I tried.

My kids and I played cards a lot during those three long years. When I won, I felt some sense of accomplishment. It was like being five years old all over again. At the time, my life's purpose was merely to survive each day, which was extremely challenging, but playing cards with my kids brought me some semblance of joy. They also amazed me with the wise things that would come out of their mouths. My daughter, Kennedy, was only nine when I started going through my health crisis. I would do my best to snuggle with her at bed time. Her wise little soul would have insights for me as to why it was all happening. She'd ponder, "Maybe you are supposed to feel this way, Mom, so you can understand what other people go through." And, "Maybe you are supposed to learn how to help other people with these problems." I would lie in her bed and look into her sweet blue eyes and melt inside. The way I felt was not the way I wanted my daughter to see me. It was not the way I thought it was supposed to be. I wanted to play with her and take her places. I wanted to participate in her life, but I just couldn't be in public. I could hardly stand each day in my house, as it was. I cried uncontrollably all the time. My kids witnessed that, too. Besides playing games for entertainment, I spent my time expressing my pain through poems, which became a cathartic practice for me. Kennedy at age nine, bless her heart, decided she wanted to write one, too. It sure did put a smile on my face.

LOVE
by Kennedy Kantor (age 9)

I love the way my family plays
I love the way we say what we think we know,
My family can fight but it comes down to that I am right
We get along in a unique way
But we are happy everyday
So to my family I'll say
I love the way we are, so be yourself everyday!

My compromised health became the norm to my family, but for me, I was getting more and more angry and agitated the longer my condition persisted. Thankfully, my eldest son, Sammy, was a huge support. During many of my most desperate moments, he would insist upon doing something with me that would distract me from my misery. He would push me to take a walk with him, or to play catch with him in the backyard, or to simply sit with him and have a conversation, all of which were successful tactics that got me to stop crying, at least for a period of time. Even though Sammy was a teenager, he took time out of his high school social life to help his siblings with life necessities that I was not capable of helping them with. He would drive them to their activities, help them with homework and care for them when they were sick or sad. I will forever be grateful for all of his love and support when I needed it most.

After returning from HHI, I felt a slight improvement in my health for about a week, but then things started spiraling downhill again. Away from my safe, healing retreat oasis, I began to experience intense anxiety and physical pain all the time again, along with increased sensitivities to TV, lights and smells. I felt like a turtle without its shell - so vulnerable, fragile, unsafe and raw. Our house was usually kept dark for my comfort level, for when I would venture downstairs. While everyone else watched TV, I would lie on the couch, in my husband's lap, staring at the ceiling, just to be in the same room as my husband and children. It was bittersweet. I was so miserable, and they would be there laughing at a show or just having a normal conversation. I had become a spectator in my own life, and it was devastating. I would get myself so worked up, even jealous, thinking about not being able to participate in my own life, that I would end up retreating upstairs and listening to a podcast or some inspirational speaker, in order to soothe myself. The recordings I found brought me much needed hope; though at times, I would get agitated wondering how those speakers would handle what I was experiencing! Mine wasn't your typical *upset* that most of the inspiring leaders were speaking about. Mine was hell on earth!

Hell on earth was not void of funny moments, however. Due to a medication I was taking around that time, my testosterone was off the charts. One afternoon I insisted that my husband come upstairs to "do the deed" with me. One of my sons walked in on us and was shocked. He later chastised my husband, "Dad, don't do that to her. Isn't that bad for mom's condition?" That must have been a fun conversation for my husband to field. Doron and I laughed our asses off. Thank God for comic relief.

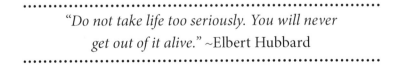

"Do not take life too seriously. You will never get out of it alive." ~Elbert Hubbard

JOY

What I look forward to at the end of each day,
Is snuggling with Kenna, our laughter and play.
Playing cards with my kids is always a treat,
Especially when it's me they are trying to beat.
The extra family time this situation has given,
Encourages me to get out of this prison.
I feel so much joy deep in my heart,
And I look forward to having a brand new start.

SCENE 16
Earth-ing Angel Abby

B eing the manager at my husband's office, Kelly really needed to get back to work. She had spent three months with me and the clinic needed her. She gave Abby a call to see if she would be available to help me for a couple of months. Besides being our kids' Hebrew teacher, Abby was a transformational life coach and also a graduate of Hippocrates Health Institute's Health Educator and Coaching Program, so we thought that with her help implementing the same healing protocol that I had learned at HHI, I would see results. Even though I disliked the idea of needing a caretaker, I will always be grateful for the time I spent with Abby. I don't think I have ever met a more enthusiastic, high energy personality. She was exactly what I needed at that point in my journey. Life was very frightening, painful and depressing. I needed a light of positivity and excitement in my environment. Enter, Abby.

Abby swooped in like a ball of light, appearing in my life like Glenda the Good Witch came to Dorothy, waving her healing wand to help guide me home out of this nightmare. Abby was a vegan health educator and chef, and she loved educating people through cooking healthy meals for them. She was so great at making me fresh squeezed juice every morning, and preparing healthy food options for my meals. She also did a lot of research on different types of healers that I could visit, and I have her to thank for introducing me to my metaphysical heroes like Deepak Chopra, Abraham Hicks and Louise L. Hay. We laughed and cried and got very close during our time together. One of my favorite days with Abby was when she drove me to Golden Gardens, a beautiful beach in Seattle, Washington. She had me take off my shoes and walk barefoot ("earth") in the sand. As I inched closer to the water, I felt a rush of joy flow through me. It was such a magical feeling, and I shouted out with hope and exhilaration, like Rocky reaching the top of the steps after his long climb. I so desperately needed those Divine moments to help me survive my situation. I felt a connection with a higher source, which inspired me to stay strong and stay the course.

Golden Gardens became my new happy place. I'd have my husband take me there when I needed to get out. I never did have the same sacred experience that I had the first time I went there with Abby, but I still felt a connection to Source, and was grateful for the beauty of the beach. Abby was very good (as was Kelly) at helping me look at the hellish Groundhog Day that I was living through as part of my journey; and she kept reminding me that there was a bigger reason for and purpose to all of it. I became deeply intrigued with finding my "purpose." That mission alone gave me the strength to continue pushing through my agony. After all, the nightmare had to be close to over, right? As miserable as I felt, Abby would get me up and take me on hikes, even if it was for a short jaunt, just to get me out in nature.

I know that all of her efforts with diet and encouragement helped me through the days we spent together, but towards the end of Abby's time with me, I could see that I wasn't getting any better. Again, the frustration, upset and worry crept in, and I felt that all too familiar feeling of hopelessness and being totally lost. There was talk of another caretaker coming to replace Abby, and I just shrunk with disappointment. I was a grown woman with three kids and a husband, yet the discussion at hand was about getting me another caretaker, as no one, including myself, felt comfortable with leaving me alone. One of my husband's patients, Michelle, who was a caretaker for the elderly, was in-between jobs and happened to be available to help me. I felt broken-hearted that I wasn't capable of living life on my own. I was suffering immeasurably everyday, and I felt like I couldn't take it anymore.

••

"The secret of living well is not in having all of the answers but in pursuing unanswerable questions in good company." ~Rachel Naomi Remen

••

UNIVERSE

I trust that You'll guide me, so this condition I'll beat,
Bring my body its balance and get me back on my feet.

I want to help others who struggle like me,
Give them comfort and hope that they may not see.

I have lots of plans, so please give me the chance,
To feel free in my body, to sing, play and dance.

I'm getting so antsy and it's so hard to wait,
I really want to believe great health is my fate.

Please give me the answers I desperately need,
I trust You will guide me and I will succeed.

SCENE 17
Forced to Find My Voice

I can't begin to tell you how infuriated I felt about my experience day in and day out. My body was so deprived of sleep and the physical, emotional and mental symptoms I was experiencing were unbearable. I continued to cry out of desperation, pleading to God to save me from my agony. I had been to countless doctors at this point. I had spent so much money. I begrudgingly shared my story so many times. I had gotten my hopes up with each subsequent visit to every "health professional," that I was finally with the "expert" who was going to figure it all out. And still, after one and a half years of suffering with my mystery illness, I had nothing - no diagnosis, no answers, no relief. Life was flying by me. I always loved watching birds as they soar in their v-shaped patterns. They travel in-sync to catch the preceding bird's updraft, which helps them fly. I felt like that one lone bird who just couldn't keep up. I was out of sync with my flock. I was missing events, trips, special occasions and even simple things like going to the store or to the movies with my friends and family. My kids were moving on with their lives without me. The irony, though, was that I was far more dependent on them than they were on me. The paradox of that role reversal devastated me. Although I was in awe of their independence and responsibility, I wondered if I'd ever be able to synchronize back into my family and life as a functional wife and mother. I dreamed of reintegrating back into formation and rejoining my flock with stronger wings.

We were referred to another chiropractor who specialized in neurology. He was referred to us based on his success with helping to heal head injuries. He was young and seemed kind and warm at first, but his demeanor changed quickly; he became very focused and serious after a short time. I would go to him without much sleep, and spend hours doing different exercises in his office, so that he could study my eyes and my gait. Executing the tasks he had me perform were hard work for me, and required a lot of patience. Even the mere word "patience" started to agitate me. One and a half years of dealing with what I was going through, was *beyond* patience. I was fragile and vulnerable. The doctor was very proud of his own work, and would get very frustrated with me if he didn't like the way I was doing an exercise, or when I would repeat my concerns about my relentless symptoms, judging me for sounding negative. He was used to seeing better results in his patients (or so he made sure to inform me, many times). His ego could not stand seeing me take longer than expected to improve. He actually yelled at me one day, and I couldn't hold back the tears. I was shocked by his bedside manner and came to feel affronted. He was one of the only doctors in the area doing that specific healing work, and we really felt that it was helping my brain injury. I chose to continue working with him despite my personal discomfort around him.

Every trying situation has a silver lining, though. Working with this gruff doc helped me find my voice. Working with him was a definite turning point for me. Being in such a raw, vulnerable state completely silenced my ego, abolishing all of my lifelong fears of being judged. From that place, I felt a confidence that I had not ordinarily experienced, which allowed me to express myself effectively and to "finally" stand up for myself (to some degree). In my desperate state, I felt like I had nothing to hide or to lose by being my most authentic self. I ended up sending that doctor an email letting him know that I expected more understanding and patience from him if we were to continue working together. Sending that message to him represented me putting my first toe on the ground along my journey towards standing up on my own two feet. I noticed the next morning during our appointment that the doctor's demeanor had shifted, and as a result, the sessions became better. It confirmed for me how important and effective it truly was to use my own voice. I credit that health practitioner for helping me to improve and for working on healing my CTE (Chronic Traumatic Encephalopathy). That said, my journey was far from over.

During one of our sessions, I ended up getting a case of vertigo, and the chiropractor tried different techniques to help rebalance the "crystals" in my ear. The utricle is a part of the ear which contains calcium crystals called canaliths, helping the ear detect movement. If the crystals become detached from the utricle and end up inside the semicircular ear canals, when they move, they can send misleading signals to the brain about one's physical position, causing vertigo. It was a very unpleasant experience, and I remember thinking that I couldn't believe that trying to overcome vertigo was yet another addition to my torturous reality. Just when I thought things couldn't get worse... they did. My only outings were to doctors' offices and the grocery store, where I would wait in the car and try to keep the world from spinning while someone else did the shopping. My painful existence was non-stop, flat out torture with no breaks. I often wondered when the life I was experiencing would finally turn around, allowing all of the horror to become a thing of the past. I questioned many times if I should push on. I knew that if it didn't get better, I wouldn't make it much longer. No one could live like this. I knew in my heart that I couldn't, anyway.

"Holding on to hope when everything is dark, is the greatest test of faith." ~Yamin Mogahed

SCENE 18
Can't See the Light

finally stopped seeing the doctor who made me so uncomfortable, and moved on to seeking out the next possible treatment that I prayed would be my saving grace.

So many recommendations for different practitioners and protocols were coming at me all the time, from so many different sources, that there was no way to explore them all at once. I had been referred to the Amen Clinic in Bellevue, Washington a while back, and after cutting ties with the harsh chiropractor, I made my way there. With a name like *Amen*, I expected to finally get some heavenly intervention. I went to my first appointment and again, like so many times before, I repeated my ever-deepening story to the new doc, which always took a lot out of me. He seemed very knowledgeable, and I felt hopeful that I had at last found salvation. Amen! This would be it for me.

I had a good first meeting with the doctor, and I was scheduled to come back for brain scans on two different days. I had to lie perfectly still for each scanning session, where they injected me with a radioactive formula. The tests were long and challenging, but once again, I got into my zone and allowed them to ensue. The Amen doc went over his findings with me. I had indeed sustained brain damage on my frontal lobe along with a couple of other areas. The results came as no surprise to me considering the constant sensations of tightness, pressure, buzzing and moments of intense lightning bolt like pain shooting through my brain. I was also extremely sensitive to lights, scents, and sounds. The left frontal lobe controls the muscles on the right side of the body, while the right frontal lobe controls the muscles on the left. My gait showed signs that the right side of my body was not receiving complete information from my frontal lobe. When I would walk, my right arm would not move in sync with my legs. I would also experience involuntary shaking of my limbs, which also conveyed the dysfunction of the brain's messaging system. The hypothalamus-pituitary-adrenal (HPA) controls the release of cortisol into the bloodstream. I was experiencing off-the-charts levels of cortisol in my body, further confirming the imbalance in my brain. More damage was found in my Amygdala - part of the limbic system that deals with emotional responses including the fight or flight response. This made sense to me, as I almost always felt as though I was looking a tiger in the eye. The doctor's findings validated the symptoms I had been experiencing, though they did not change my desperate desire for relief. He prescribed supplements for me and we discussed an optimal diet for brain health. I was again hopeful that in a month or so I would be noticing change. Another recommendation from the Amen Clinic was for me to be fitted for certain glasses with colored lenses that were said to calm the brain. They referred me to the lady they worked with, Terry, and she turned out to be another angel along my journey.

As I mentioned, my senses were extremely heightened. Not only could I not tolerate any light besides daylight, but I had a very hard time around pungent smells, from perfume to paint. And I never knew what would set me off. I became paranoid to go out of my house for fear of being triggered - that someone might be wearing a strong perfume, or that the lights in a doctor's office would be too bright. I walked around in brutal discomfort all the time, because inevitably, as soon as I stepped out of my comfort zone, *something* would affect me. I developed massive empathy for children with autism and other sensory issues. The special glasses promised to give me some relief when I was exposed to artificial light, thus allowing me to go more places without being as negatively affected. There was an overwhelming array of different colored shades to choose from - probably upwards of a hundred - so trying to find a pair that worked best was a long, frustrating process. My brain became confused trying on so many colors, one after another, so it was extremely challenging for me to decipher, through my discomfort, whether any of them were working. I pushed through, believing that if I took the time to explore that and *any* protocol, I may receive the benefits of my efforts. It was always a major let down, however, when I would put in the time and get no results.

"Rainbow Glasses Lady Terry" was so very kind, compassionate and caring towards me and my situation. She really wanted to help me find solace. I spent two to three hours at a time, on many different occasions, trying on different combinations of filters, trying to find any inkling of relief. Once in a while, I would experience some calming effect and think to myself, "Wow, this is going to be good!" But then, when I would try that same filter again, I wouldn't experience the same reprieve. After many hours of working with Terry, both at her office and at my home, I came to realize that the colored lens therapy would not work for me, and it was time to let it go. It was such a huge disappointment each time any seemingly hopeful protocol didn't work. We had tried so many outlets, spent countless hours and doled out ridiculous amounts of money… for nothing to bring me the comfort I so desperately needed.

My situation put life itself into perspective. I, like all of us, have been faced with many choices in different circumstances throughout my life - which job to choose, which house to buy, which person to marry, or not to marry... and no matter what decisions I made, the outcomes were exactly what they were supposed to be, no matter how doubtful I was of my choices. Those decisions that I was called to make, however, were not "life or death" decisions. My situation literally felt like life or death to me. I had two choices: to continue to live in excruciating pain or to end my life. I was intensely aware of the other times when I was confronted with tough decisions that felt like "life or death" to me at the time. In my condition, I would have begged to go through the upset of getting fired, the disappointment of being denied my offer on a house or the heartache of a break-up over my brain injury. Disappointments, upsets and rejections are life-altering and heartbreaking, true; but I knew from experience that they wouldn't drive me over the edge. Those conflicted options would have been more manageable for me than the pain I was living with, which made me want to just check out for good. Life is truly all about perspective.

I became increasingly concerned that I'd never find an answer, and I knew damn well that I could not and would not live my life like I had been living - incapacitated by my excruciating condition. I was so drained and disheartened by it all. I kept reminding myself that I had three kids and I could *not* bail on them. I also knew that I couldn't handle the constant pain I was in for much longer. I felt stuck between a rock and a hard place. Neither decision was acceptable at all. It was beyond critical that I start healing, and fast.

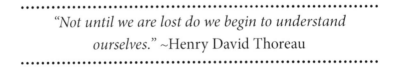

"Not until we are lost do we begin to understand ourselves." ~Henry David Thoreau

BELIEVE

It's been almost two years, that I've been in this state,
Each day without relief makes it harder to wait.
I keep on believing that healing is almost here,
But when it doesn't show up, it gets harder not to fear.
My nervous system is so heightened, all my senses too,
It's getting harder and harder for me to keep my cool.
How long must I wait to get what I need?
I scream and I cry, I beg and I plead.
I picture my life with peace, joy and fun,
I need a vacation in the healing sun.
You never get to know what is coming your way,
I highly recommend that you enjoy each day.
Sometimes things happen, then we aren't quite the same,
Our world becomes challenging, it's really quite a shame.
Please don't sweat the small stuff and appreciate the good,
Don't dismiss your blessings, acknowledge them you should.

SCENE 19
Falling Fast

've heard it said that when evolving, one must "get comfortable with being uncomfortable," and that discomfort is a sign of growth. While that might be true, during my struggle, I wanted to punch whoever said that in the face. Learning how to be comfortable in my discomfort was impossible for me. I didn't need to grow that much. The doctor at the Amen Clinic had recommended that part of my treatment involve sitting in hyperbaric chambers - every day - with forty visits in a row, minimum, just to start. Forty *minimum* was right. Little did I know, forty visits would turn into *one hundred*! Hyperbaric chambers are known for improving and even healing many different illnesses. Unfortunately, though, they are oxygen-infused *coffins*. I get claustrophobic in small areas. It really made me feel for coal miners. Not only did I feel trapped in my own body, but now, once a day, I "got" to feel trapped inside of a steel coffin with only one peephole. The chamber was a metal tank that I was locked in for an hour and fifteen minutes. I wore a clear plastic, pail-shaped contraption over my entire head, face and neck, with tubes that connected to the head piece, and carried the oxygen in and out of the device. I had already been dealing with so much for so long, when the claustrophobic chamber experience entered stage right. Once again, I told myself to just stick with it, as it might bring me the relief for which I had been longing for so long. I tried to envision myself as a caterpillar in a cocoon, who had to do her time in order to be ready to fly her way to freedom. Even though I felt more and more defeated with every failed treatment, I had an inexplicable desire to keep pushing forward. I felt that I deserved a metamorphosis, to transform to the other side of whatever was afflicting me, since I had already put in so much time and had suffered so much. The hyperbaric chamber was scary at first, but as time went by, I got used to it. Hell, I'd get used to anything if it meant that I could feel well again - well enough not to need a chaperone or a driver!

It didn't matter who my "driver" was on my appointment outings, I found it hard to talk with anyone, as I used all my energy to stabilize myself enough so that I didn't have a panic attack or break down crying. My brain injury had created the most agonizing sensations, like a hammer smashing my head over and over, constantly. Coupled with the sleep deprivation, my emotions were fragile and raw. I felt that way every single day. I felt so badly for Michelle, who was my "chaperone" at the time, because it was a struggle to hold any conversation with her. Sometimes after arriving at my hyperbaric sessions, I was so fragile that Michelle had to help me walk inside. Other times, I would have her sit in the chamber with me, bless her heart. Michelle was very calm, loving and hopeful for my recovery. I deeply appreciated our insightful and spiritual conversations (when I was able to hold one with her), and I wholeheartedly know that our paths were meant to cross, as we both had wisdom to share with one another and growth to experience together. She was a wonderful help and I still feel badly about our final days together.

One day, as I got out of the car in front of my hyperbaric chamber appointment, I had a full-blown panic attack. I really thought I was dying. I asked her to get a friend of mine who worked in the same building because I really needed to see someone familiar. When he came out, I hugged him as if I had just a few minutes left to live. I was hysterical and terrified. I knew he must have been thinking I was crazy, but I really didn't care. If I were going to die, I wanted someone I knew with me. They took me inside to try and calm me down. Embarrassment would have been a reasonable feeling coming from the old me, but I was so far beyond caring about how anyone perceived me at that juncture. I was fighting to keep calm and to hold it together. I think my last interaction with Michelle was when she drove me to yet another appointment in Issaquah. We were early so we took a little walk in a shaded area surrounded by trees. My brain was extra distorted that day, and I was feeling unstable and frightened. Sometimes things got so intense that, again, I thought I might die. I was crying and hollering, "I just want my kids!" I had her drive me home. I was really melting down, and I think that was her last straw.

It was so hard to be with me without getting emotionally affected. My thirteen and fifteen-year-old boys were home when we pulled up, and they helped me into the house, all too familiar with what was happening, and assuring Michelle, "We got this." I think at that point Michelle was in tears, too. She just didn't know how to help me. She wasn't alone; most people felt the same way. Shortly after that experience, Michelle let my husband know that she wasn't able to help out anymore. Shocker. I didn't blame her. It was nice that she stayed as long as she did. She was a gentle soul with a kind, warm heart who had a passion for helping others. I am grateful that she came to care for me as long as she did. We totally understood, but then there was no one to stay with me all day. I wasn't in any shape to be left alone, so my husband had to work a new plan. He asked his parents if they would be willing to stay with me at our house and take me to my appointments on certain days. They lovingly agreed. Even though I despised the way I was feeling, I really enjoyed the bonding time with my mother-in-law. I would snuggle up to her like a puppy with its pack, and she would share stories with me about her childhood and family relationships. We believed we must have been related in a past life. After all, we did share the same maiden name and my husband would often say, "I married my mother." Sometimes when my father-in-law and mother-in-law would come over, I was jealous when they would take their afternoon snoozes on the couch while they were "babysitting" me. All I wanted was to be in their slippers, snoring my cares away, unconscious of my painful reality. I will always appreciate their love and support during this tumultuous time.

"If you want to make God laugh, tell Him about your plans." ~Woody Allen

SCENE 20
A Grudge with God

....

*"The biggest obstacle you'll ever have to overcome
is your mind. If you can overcome that, you
can overcome anything."* ~Les Brown

....

T he way I looked on the outside was incongruent to how much I was suffering on the inside. My raging symptoms were constant. I felt like a rusty knitting needle was being poked incessantly at the back of my eyeballs. I would do my best to stay calm and focused and to get into my "zen zone" whenever I went to see doctors or when anyone other than my immediate family came for a visit. I wanted to make those encounters as productive and non-dramatic as possible. Once I was alone again, I would lose my shit. Even when my older brother would stop by to see me, I felt the need to hide my symptoms, as I didn't want him to judge me as his "crazy, frantic sister." I was like that singing frog from a cartoon I used to watch as a child, where the frog would sing and dance for his human friend, then in front of an audience he would just sit still and ribbit. My husband used to get angered by the deception of my more composed representation of myself, because it wasn't the entire picture of the frantic way I was behaving at home. He was concerned that the doctors could not see exactly what was wrong if I were holding it together so well at every visit. He was also disturbed that our friends and family couldn't possibly understand what I was going through, either, since they never saw that side of me.

I was often told that head injuries can take months and even years to heal, and sadly, I can vouch for that. That was also hard for people to grasp. I wasn't a football player or a boxer, so how could I have been so affected by a fall? When you research the brain and how fragile it truly is, though, you start to understand that it doesn't take much to damage it. Even a mild bump or abrasion to the brain can cause bruising and cortisol levels to skyrocket, which can lead to aggressive symptoms like the ones I experienced for three long years; from being in a constant state of fight-or-flight to persistent insomnia, to vertigo to severe depression. Even though I had merely tripped while jogging and whiplashed my head, since it was my fourth brain injury, I had clearly done enough harm to cause major damage. The questions became: would I ever heal? And if so, how long would it take?

When a year would go by and I was still the same for the most part, but worse from the stress and strain that I had undergone, I would get very frightened and wonder if this was it for me. Sometimes, I would become extremely angry and scream and yell at God. I felt so betrayed by that supposedly benevolent force who wanted the best for everyone. I understood that bad things happened to people all the time, but I also felt like the suffering I had endured was enough already. I would lay in my bed and ask God to take me if this was the way it was going to be. I would rather be out of my physical body than live with so much pain.

Oftentimes, I would be angry and bitter in my requests to God, but at other times I was accepting and calm, and would surrender to the fact that I had experienced a very good life with wonderful people and experiences, and was "ready to go, please." I knew I couldn't live a happy, comfortable life in my condition, and I was accepting of moving on. Much of the spiritual content that I was listening to daily made the "other side" sound quite lovely, actually, and I was past due for "quite lovely". I just felt that it was supposed to be God's job to make my transition happen, not mine. Why should I take my own life and look like a quitter to my friends and family, and especially to my kids? I would have chats with my oldest son trying to explain that I didn't want to leave my family, but I couldn't handle what I was feeling much longer. In retrospect, it probably wasn't the smartest thing to talk to my kids about that, but I am OK with the fact that I did. I strongly believe in being open and honest with my kids, and I think it empowers them when they understand that I believe in them and in their ability to handle anything. I strongly needed their support, and my trauma was glaringly obvious, not even something that I could hide from them. There were a few occasions when I acted in ways that I wish I could do over, but I have also forgiven myself for those times, as I was struggling immensely.

As time slinked by with no relief, I started to have thoughts encouraging me to end my misery. One day, in that state, I was very angry and I'd had enough. I marched into the kitchen where my middle son, Nathan, was standing. I opened the knife drawer, put my hand on a knife and snarled out loud to myself, "Do it already!" as if the real me didn't have the guts. It was a cry for help. As young as he was, Nathan was wise enough to understand my dramatic act out. Nate always responded appropriately. He used humor as his mechanism to handle me in that instance. He chuckled and said, "Stop it, mom!" He tried to act like he was unfazed by my antics, even though he was traumatized. He comforted me to diffuse the situation, hiding any fear he had. He then walked me up to my room and stayed there with me until my husband got home.

Another frightening instance happened one afternoon, again with Nathan around, while I attempted to take a nap. Anytime I was able to doze off was a godsend. I wish I could have just "napped" through those entire three years! I was actually able to doze off on this particular day, but was startled awake with major spinning and anxiety racing through my head and body. I couldn't move very well and started screaming for Nathan to come help me. When he came in, I fell to the floor and started hanging on him and begging him to save me. I thought I was dying, again. It still blows me away to think about what the brain and body are capable of. Again, my poor eleven-year-old son had his mom wigging out with no adults around. And again, he played it cool and assured me, "You are fine, mom!" Bless his heart. I will forever admire the strength my children possessed, especially having to witness their mom suffer every day.

*"Expect the unexpected, life is not meant to be easy.
We all have our challenges. It's how we respond
to them that really matters."* ~Peter Waite

SCENE 21
Don't Believe Everything They Tell You

··

"Maybe life isn't about avoiding the bruises,
but about collecting the scars to prove we
showed up for it." ~Theresa Buszta

··

One of the many recommendations I was given was for a physical therapist (PT) who specialized in treating specific cervical nerve problems. Let me back-up. I was seeing a doctor for cranial sacral work and he took an X-ray of my neck. Based on the problem he saw in the X-ray, he felt that I was a candidate for the healing work this PT did, and apparently she was the best at treating it. I was a bit shocked when I first met her. She had a very serious and dry personality. She was rigid and said it like she saw it, without much warmth or connection involved. Very Cruella DeVille, and I did not like being one of her dalmations. Feeling as fragile as a wounded bird, I could have used some T.L.C. Unfortunately, that's not how she rolled. She went over the details of the work she could do with me, but that was before she had even seen my X-rays. It ended up taking awhile for her to get them, and I recall her sending me back to get yet another CAT-scan so we could move things along.

I wasn't a big fan of confining places or of sitting perfectly still for long periods of time, and I was in no form to do either; but again, I wanted answers and results, so I did what "the experts" said needed to be done. It took a lot of strength for me to be jammed into the uncomfortable CAT-scan machine, but I am proud of myself for pushing through when I didn't think I had it in me anymore. To distract myself while I sat and waited for the process to be over, I daydreamed of a magical future. Keeping a positive attitude was all I really had going for me and it was inspiring to think about "living it up" when the time came... if it came.

When she finally received and analyzed my scans, PT Cruella scared the spots off my back as she delivered the devastating news about my condition. She compared me to others with the same neck issue she claimed I had, and made it sound like I'd need surgery in my neck if it didn't improve from her exercises. I could not believe it. Part of me wanted to give up on life right there, but the other part of me, who felt like I had been running an exasperating marathon, did not want to quit on mile twenty-one. The longer I pushed through the discomfort of mere living, the more deserving I felt I was of getting better, and I was determined to keep running. I mean, why bother putting myself through so much torture, as I had for the past two years, if only to give up on myself? But I was burning out and didn't have much energy to continue. They say the biggest struggles bring about the best rewards, but what kind of a reward was neck surgery?

New surprises kept showing up in my life during that traumatic time. The PT's frightening analysis of my scans, in addition to the physical reaction from the tests that I underwent, per the PT's request, were some of those unwelcome surprises. The CAT-scan brought about yet another negative effect on my brain. I already had an extreme sensitivity to artificial light, then after the scan, it suddenly became unbearable for me to open my eyes without excruciating discomfort, outside in *daylight*. After subjecting myself to those tests, I found myself stuck in my dark room for four days with the ticking time bomb inside my head. Even in the worst of times, though, we must be able to laugh at our situations. Sometimes I would chuckle and say,

"Nice one, God!" My chuckling would quickly turn into sobbing and frustration but it was nice to see I still had a sense of humor. Abby was with me during that time, and I'm grateful she was. She really helped me realize that I didn't need to believe everything the PT was saying, however confidently she was saying it. After working with that PT three days a week for two months, and getting no results, I realized her protocol wasn't my answer… neither was her diagnosis.

"Look inside yourself for the answers - you are the only one who knows what's best for you. Everybody else is only guessing." ~Charles de Lint

SCENE 22
Shoot Me Up

As intense as my symptoms were to me, my husband's loyalty matched them.

Having my partner in life by my side to share my struggle was the greatest comfort I could have ever hoped for. My husband was born in South Africa. I was set up with him by some mutual friends. When he called me for the first time, I was totally enchanted by his accent. We spoke for forty-five minutes and I happily let him do most of the talking. I just wanted to listen to him speak. He came to the States at thirteen years old, and had never returned to South Africa since. His parents and siblings lived close to us. We had been married for years when his parents expressed their desire for the whole family to travel to South Africa together. We had booked tickets a year into my injury, and I was certain I would be healed by the time we were supposed to go the following year. I had already missed so many holidays, family functions, school events and more. Our trip was approaching and we had to make a final decision about whether or not I should go.

It was quite clear that there was no way I could go in the condition I was in, and Doron refused to leave me in the care of anyone else. My outbreaks were quite intense and no one else would know how to handle them. His family wasn't very happy about his choice to stay behind with me, and I felt super guilty for keeping him from finally making it back to his homeland, but he wouldn't budge on his decision to stay with me. Talk about loyalty. Again, I was so very disappointed that I couldn't go with my kids on that trip. I felt like life was happening all around me, but I couldn't participate. I knew I would never get that time back. I felt helpless and in despair. I kept asking, "WHY?," but never felt answered. The more I turned inward and found forgiveness and understanding for my past, the more frustrating it became to not advance in my physical healing. All of my spiritual teachers said that if I healed my soul and forgave myself and all who hurt me, my physical healing would follow. And yet, there I still was, captive in my pain. I suppose I still had more lessons to learn.

My husband planned to use the time that the family was away wisely, and arranged to fly me to Arizona to have a stem cell procedure. He had done a lot of research on stem cells and the healing effects they could have on the body. He was hopeful that the procedure would speed up the recovery of my brain. Getting me through the airport with all the lights and smells was familiarly challenging. Again, I pushed myself through the discomfort in the hopes that what lay ahead would be the answer for me, to move past my pain and flourish. My symptoms were especially flaring during that trip, which made it bittersweet: I was finally out of the house and on a "vacation" with my husband, but I couldn't enjoy it at all.

When we arrived in Arizona, engulfed by warm sun, the warrior in me wanted to disregard my symptoms and tell them to fuck off so that I could enjoy some of the majestic outdoors. I asked Doron to take me on a hike. It was lovely to be outside in nature doing something I enjoyed, but the hike was too much for me. I broke down crying on the path with an unwanted audience of gawking strangers. It felt uncomfortable to be such a wreck around people. I felt so fragile and defeated. Life hit me smack in the face, showing me that I could not even enjoy the most mundane of "normal" life activities with any semblance of contentment. During times like those, where my limitations were spotlighted, the thought of giving up would creep into my mind, as that seemed like the only way out.

Every second of every hour was slow and brutal. It was grueling to be in the hotel room, suffering on the bed, while Doron sprawled out comfortably watching TV. There was nothing he could do for me, but my dire need for help felt as urgent as if the room were on fire. I was in survival mode, yet I was watching him do nothing. It was such a mind fuck! My inner world felt urgent and tragic, while the world around me looked calm and "normal." I would try and listen to podcasts to move time, but it was a struggle. I'd daydream about my kids having a blast in South Africa and wondered what I'd be doing if I were with them. Would I be holding a baby tiger or taking photos of a zebra giving birth? Who knew? I'd never know.

I was injected with one round of the stem cell infusion, which took a few hours. The doctors were hopeful and very confident that their treatment would help me based on the success stories of their previous clients. They informed me that the treatment could take anywhere from a few days to a few months to show any positive results. I was praying for the former. If I could be on the mend when my kids returned from their journey abroad, that would be the biggest blessing I could ever imagine. Again, I got my hopes up that The Universe led me to the doctors in Arizona to find my saving grace. However, after many months with no improvement in my condition, I realized that, no surprise, the stem cell infusion wasn't my cure. I strove even harder to live up to Nietzche's words, "To live is to suffer. To survive is to find some meaning in the suffering." I dove deeper into my spiritual teachings to try and find some meaning in mine.

••

"Sometimes you have to get knocked down
lower than you have ever been to stand back
up taller than you ever were." ~Unknown

••

SCENE 23
Intruders! Intruders!

I waited at least a month to get in to see Dr. Dan. He specialized in a technique called Neurological Integration System (NIS). The purpose of NIS is to use the brain to optimize the function and repair of the body. When I finally got in to see him, I found out that I was dealing with parasites on top of everything else. Nothing could faze me at that point. It wasn't a question of whether more obstacles would be put in my way; it was a question of *what* would be the next hurdle? I was used to the chaos already. Dr. Dan explained that when the immune system is down, bacteria, viruses and even parasites can attack the body and wreak havoc, so it was important to clean up the creepy crawlers. Dr. Dan had suffered intensely from parasites in the past, and after experiencing healing with the NIS technique, he decided to get trained in it so that he could help others. A man after my own heart. Unfortunately, Dr. Dan was completely booked. He was very busy helping people, and it would take another week or two to see him again. He referred me to Dr. Kurt, whose healing practice, including NIS, was located thirty minutes from where I lived. I was able to get in and see him a few times each week. Dr. Kurt was amazing - very kind and patient with me. He went above and beyond, spending extra time, and doing his darndest to try and find me the relief for which I begged. I think every protocol I tried, including NIS, must have contributed in its own way to my healing, but I just wasn't feeling any of the positive effects. I was not improving. Again, I was told by Dr. Kurt that it took a very long time for the brain to create new pathways in order to heal itself.

I enjoyed going to Dr. Kurt's office. It was the highlight of my days. He and his staff were all so caring and friendly. It was always a pleasure going to see them. I got a referral from them for a homeopathic doctor, Dr. Steven, who they said had helped many people over the years. I gave him a call and we had a great conversation. We set up an appointment for the following week. He had a cute office attached to his home. My symptoms were so extreme that I had to lie down on his bench while he did his patient intake with me. I couldn't remain in an upright position for long periods of time or I'd begin to feel unbearable pressure in my head. I also felt more fatigued when standing upright, so lying down was the best position for me. Dr. Steven and I must have talked for more than two hours during that first visit. He needed as much detail about my past and about my current situation as possible, and it took quite some time for me to explain it all. I cried uncontrollably in bursts during that time in his office, as I was in so much physical pain. I prayed that he would choose the right remedy for me on the first try.

After he gave me the herbal tincture, I immediately went home and jumped into bed, hoping to finally embrace sleep. Dr. Steven said that some people actually sleep for many hours right after taking the remedy, no matter what time of day. Being that lack of sleep was one of my main conditions, I was very excited to see if I would have the same luck as his other patients upon taking the tincture. Even a day of sleep would give me *some* temporary relief. Unfortunately, I wasn't that lucky. I had a switch that was turned on in my brain and it wasn't about to switch off with some tincture. I don't even think that the apple Snow White ate would knock me out. I called Dr. Steven for consolation. I spoke with him many times over the phone. He was kind and understanding. I really believed in him, but again, it was so hard for me to stick around and see if I would get results from a protocol that clearly wasn't working from the start. After trying six different remedies from Dr. Steven, I realized that, for whatever was going on in my brain, herbs were not going to be the panacea. While I'm sure the herbs contributed to my wellness on some level, I did not experience any relief from the symptoms caused by my head injury. After a few months of giving Dr. Steven's protocol a try, I realized it was time to move on.

A friend then referred me to a naturopathic doctor named Dr. Wells. She was extremely warm and engaging and I felt like she was truly invested in helping me get the answers I had longed for after so much time. After repeating my story and condition to her, she came up with a promising plan. She performed blood tests on me as well as bacteria/viral tests, and discovered that I was dealing with a high level of the Epstein Barr virus - shocker! The short of it, thank you Google, is: "The Epstein-Barr virus, formally called Human Gammaherpesvirus, is one of the nine known human herpesvirus types in the herpes family, and is one of the most common viruses in humans. It is best known as the cause of infectious mononucleosis." Some refer to mono as "the kissing virus," most likely to be caught at any and every college campus across the country. OK, I admit it, I had mono while I was in college. I flew home for a while to recover, and when I walked off the plane my mom had a look of horror on her face, not only because I looked deathly ill from Mono, but because I had also gained the "freshman fifteen." Thank you cheap beer and pizza! The Epstein-Barr virus can lay dormant in the body for years until a person becomes severely stressed, then it will often rear its ugly head, which is exactly what happened to me.

My sleeping Epstein-Barr giant had been awakened, once again, due to the extreme stress that I was under from my head injury. My blood test results confirmed that in a major way. The benign blood test range for Epstein-Barr to exist in the body without wreaking havoc is zero through nine. My results came back at 150 *plus*, which meant that my levels of the virus could be anywhere from 151 to 700! Whatever the case, the levels of Epstein-Barr in my body were OFF THE CHARTS. That virus had been awakened within me and had made itself far too comfortable for far too long. It had taken its toll on me. It was high time to show it who was boss, and get my life back.

••
"Time is a great healer and revealer." ~Unknown
••

SCENE 24
Thunder Down Under

*"Just when you think you've hit rock
bottom, you realize you're standing on
another trap door." ~*Marisha Pessl

found myself in a very raw state during the three years I spent in agony with my brain injury. Living in such profound pain allowed me to feel closer to others, as all my guards were down. I felt like a newborn chickling having just broken out of her shell, exposed and vulnerable. The severity of the agony was so intense that it superseded my former worries of being judged or not being liked. As a result, I was able to be my most vulnerable and authentic self. I met many wise people along my journey and appreciated their compassion and support. With each new introduction, I would wonder if it was the beginning of a new friendship or mentorship for me. I would hope when meeting each new person that he or she would be my godsend.

Early in my ordeal, the idea of writing a book (and even its title) came to me as part of my purpose - to share my nightmare and to help others through theirs. I would imagine writing about each of the practitioners I met, and describing the roles they played in my story. It gave me hope to envision pushing through my pain and coming out the other side well enough to tell about it. My kids would even play along with that visualization, in funny and creative ways, to help distract me from my reality. We had fun suggesting what actors would play us in the movie based on my story. I quickly picked my favorite actress, Sandra Bullock, to play moi. I love her movies and the kind of person I believe her to be - smart, strong, compassionate, open, authentic and very generous. She would portray me brilliantly. A lot of people think my husband, Doron, looks like Bradley Cooper, so we chose Bradley to play Doron. Speculating about the details of the movie about me - us - overcoming my trauma was something fun to do during the storm we were in. And we actually came up with a killer cast!

Because I looked somewhat fine on the outside but was suffering on the inside, I would often excessively share with my family and close friends about the intense, constant pain I suffered. I desperately wanted them to understand what was going on inside of me, so I would describe my symptoms in a play-by-play fashion, much too often. It was obsessive, panicky and hard for them to continue listening to… but they did. Sometimes they would feel so helpless and frustrated that they would get mad at me. This would make me feel even more crushed. I wasn't trying to upset them. I felt powerless and couldn't fix my symptoms. I wanted to run away, and yet there was nowhere to go. Often in the depths of my despair, I felt like I was in Alice in Wonderland - no potion would fix me and no door led to sanity or relief.

There was a time when one of my many doctors wanted me to try some new medications. It was far into the game, so I was not going to fight the medicine thing any longer, even though I'd had bad reactions in the past. He put me on Trazodone. Well, that backfired on me in a brutal way. I came down with priapism from that medication. If you aren't aware of that condition, let me give you the definition: "Persistent and painful erection of the penis." No, to be clear, I don't have a penis! Priapism occurs very rarely in women, but certain medications can cause a woman's clitoris to become engorged, which is extremely painful… and which is what happened to me. Again, I was in the ER keeling over in major pain from the priapism on top of all my other symptoms, hating life. What the hell?! Really? I couldn't believe this was happening to me.

Every time I thought that a new solution was finally going to be found, a new symptom or challenge invaded my life. How much longer was I going to have to endure this bullshit? I was a major mess with no sign of respite anywhere in sight. Quitting life was looking more and more enticing... at least for a little break, but that would be permanent, and I could not fathom that. I still had some fire left in me to push on.

The doctor looked very caught off-guard. I don't think he'd ever seen the engorged genitalia reaction before in a woman. He walked out of the room, red faced, to go write me a prescription for some new, hard core sedatives. That's when I decided to get the hell out of there. I would tough it out with my crazy new symptom, but I wasn't going to mess with even heavier drugs.

I had been seeing Dr. Steven, the homeopath, around the same time. He was the one who was most invested in my case. He had such a strong passion for his work and really took the time to research the best remedies for his clients. He never wanted to give up on me, and I will forever appreciate his concern and support. My husband contacted him when we left the ER to see if he could come up with a remedy that would help me in my current situation. We drove straight to his office. It was late at night, but he always made himself available for us. I think the herbal tinctures he gave me did help take the edge off, and eventually the "pain in my pants" did go away. I felt trapped in a nightmare - living with perpetual, disturbing symptoms in my head, insomnia, anxiety through the roof, depression, numbness, and pins and needles in my limbs - and now priapism. What I was living with felt inhuman with no sign of a happy ending.

"You never know how strong you are until being strong is your only choice." ~Bob Marley

SCENE 25
Desperate Measures

In February 2017, I was completely broken down, like a bird who attempted a window entry one too many times. I felt beat up, depleted and helpless. I had kept myself positive and hopeful for three long, drawn out and extremely painful years. I pushed myself so intensely to hang on... for seemingly nothing. Actually, I suppose it wasn't totally for nothing. I had many deep and powerful realizations during those three years of torment, when I had nothing else to do but learn and ponder. For one, thanks to all the gurus I discovered, I began to heal myself from an emotional standpoint. I evolved to feel more confident and connected with myself, even though I was still trapped inside my rundown body. Through lots of soul searching, I came to understand that it was my choice to be bitter or to be grateful for my life, no matter what my circumstances at any given time. I desired to live a long and happy life, devoid of trauma, especially for the benefit of my family.

Through my ordeal, I also came to appreciate that my husband and kids were part of an amazing extended family and friend village, with deep roots and strong bonds. That extended support system would always be there to love and embrace them. That realization brought me peace of mind, that my family would always be taken care of, with or without me. I started looking at death as just an inevitable part of the life journey. We don't get to pick how we die, unless we bring it on ourselves, but we can choose to accept that it's definitely going to happen. I knew that if my brain didn't heal, I wouldn't be able to continue on, and that the death experience would have to happen sooner than later for me… and probably by my own doing.

The movie "Concussion" was released during my dark night of the soul, and my husband watched it. He would tell people that I reminded him of the characters in the movie: the way I held my head during intense spasms, the way my facial expressions looked and the dire pleas that would continue to fly out of my mouth. No one could understand how it was possible for me to have sustained an injury as severe as those obtained by the professional football players featured in the film. I, too, agreed that it seemed odd, but I was living with the same effects, regardless. It is also true that each additional injury adds to the previous injuries, compounding the trauma. And I had experienced *four*!

I could see that my family was all out of patience, too. Everyone felt helpless and plain out of ideas. The only choices I seemed to have felt unfair and unsettling. Either I let them drug me up to a state of numbness so I didn't have to feel any pain anymore, like the characters in those old asylum movies... or I call it quits. Both options were terrifying and created angst and bewilderment. I felt very vulnerable and at my wit's end.

One day, I found myself home alone, which was unusual for my situation, and I started to experience a massive panic attack. I called on my sweet neighbor, Becky, for assistance. Becky and I had so much in common, as we were both in the midst of dark storms in our lives. Becky lived across the street, but for whatever reason, we had never met before my head injury. It was no coincidence, though, that The Universe brought us together when we needed each other most - at the beginning of my three year ordeal. We would throw pity parties for ourselves and were also shoulders for each other, sharing our pain and uplifting each other with inspiration. We were each other's confidants during our nightmares.

Even though Becky was dealing with her own life tragedy, she came to my aid when I reached out for her during my panic attack. Becky tried as best she could to help me through my melt down, but ended up calling 911, as she felt that more expert help was needed. When the police arrived, I explained to them what I was experiencing. It was such a surreal situation for me, to be feeling inside like my life was in extreme peril, and yet to witness the police officers behaving as if it was just another Monday afternoon. I can only imagine the crazy events they must encounter daily and how accustomed they must grow to them. The entire event as seen through their expressions made me feel a bit ridiculous, even though what was happening felt dire to me.

It took every ounce of strength I had to put my spiritual teachings into practice, breathe through my panic and calm down enough to answer their questions. My husband finally arrived at our home and told the police that he would take me to the ER. As we were driving down the freeway, so many frightening thoughts went racing through my mind. I was scared of being prescribed more meds, but I also couldn't bear feeling the way I had been feeling any longer. Witnessing what happened next, some would say that I had lost my mind, but let me be the first to tell you - I was quite aware of who I was, what I was doing, and how crazy it would seem to those without my symptoms.

For a half a second, as we were traveling sixty-five mph on the freeway, I opened my car door, desperately wanting to jump out. That's how badly I wanted it all to end. I felt such a devastating conflict raging inside of me: I didn't want to end my life, just the excruciating pain. My husband reached over me and pulled the door shut and then pulled the car over on the shoulder. My symptoms were unbearable. Doron called an ambulance and we waited on the side of the freeway for help to arrive. When the ambulance showed up, the EMTs put me on a stretcher and carried me into the vehicle. They proceeded with their protocol, which included an EKG to check my heart and gave me some kind of sedative. (Sidenote: If you want to get immediate attention at a hospital, I recommend arriving in an ambulance. You'll pay through the nose for it, but you won't have to wait hours to see a doctor)! By the time Doron arrived in his own car, I was smiling cheek to cheek. Whatever they had given me in the ambulance caused the intense stress in my body to melt away. All I wanted was more of *that*. Sadly, the antidote didn't last long; soon I was right back where I started.

Another terrifying day rolled around not long after the last. I was suffering more than usual, and my husband had gone past his threshold with me. He was getting angry, mostly out of helplessness, but he'd also simply had enough of being my caretaker *and* the head of the household. He wanted to support me and take care of me, but he also needed a break. Not only had he been focusing the best he could on his own work each day at his chiropractic clinic, but he had also taken over my job, becoming "Mr. Mom" with the household and the kids. It was a lot to manage, and it was wearing on him. In the midst of one of my breakdowns, he shouted in utter frustration, "What do you want me to do?!" At that moment, I knew I had to get out of the house, not only for my own recovery (you can't solve a problem from the same place it was created, right?), but also to give my family a break. Doron and I called my dad and stepmom and I begged them to help me. They said they'd make a few calls.

No treatment center in Seattle had an open room for me, so my husband and I set about visiting different ERs around town, while my parents called anyone they could think of who might be able to recommend a place for me. At each ER, we were told the same thing - that we would be taken back "very soon," but "very soon" turned into *hours*! I was mentally torturing myself trying to figure out what the best course of action would be. After what seemed like a wild goose chase with no resolution, we decided to go home and continue to tough it out until we could find a suitable place for me to go.

A few days later, we got a call from my dad with a recommendation from his doctor to take me to a mental healing treatment center in Texas called Menninger. Menninger is rated one of the best treatment facilities in the country. Everyone in my family agreed that I needed to give it a try. I decided it was going to be my last try.

••

"When you reach the end of your rope, tie a knot in it and hang on." ~Thomas Jefferson

••

SCENE 26
Hope on the Horizon

In March of 2017, my mom and stepdad offered to fly with me to Texas to help get me situated at Menninger. On the one hand, I was thrilled to be entering into a new environment, to be giving my family a break from my constant meltdowns, and most of all, to hopefully be getting the help I urgently needed. On the other hand, I felt anxious about what the Menninger program entailed and about how I would handle being without my family's support in my fragile state. The doctors at Menninger were rated top in the nation, which gave me hope, and I was desperate for them to help me.

After a long day of travelling and white knuckling it through the airport and the flight, barely able to deal with my heightened aggravation towards the lights and scents, we landed. Once outside the Houston airport, we called an Uber to take us to the treatment center. Just as my luck would have it, as soon as I opened the door, I was hit in the face with a most disturbing stench - the Uber smelled like it had been saturated in cologne; like a greasy guy with an unbuttoned shirt, hairy chest and gold chain had just bathed with an entire bottle in the back seat. It was so strong that I had to hang my head out the window like a dog during the entire drive. Those types of situations really pissed me off and made me feel like I had a dark cloud hovering over me, like Pig Pen from Charlie Brown, and I just couldn't get out from under it.

It was uncomfortable and a bit scary to be dropped off at Menninger, about to be confined to my uncertain quarters, and by *choice*. At Menninger, they made it very clear that it was the patient's commitment and choice to follow the rules and the program as best they could. Like everything I had experienced over the last three years, this, too, was utterly surreal... that I would actually be staying in a place like Menninger for an extended period of time. All because I had damaged my brain and it wasn't performing for me the way it was designed.

As we entered the building I was relieved to see that at least Menninger was a beautiful facility. That cooled my nerves a little, especially recalling my last uncomfortable stay at the sterile and gloomy hospital where I was admitted two years prior. We were given a tour, then my parents went off to meet with one of the counselors, while I was shown to what would be my room and living quarters for the next two months. It was hard to say goodbye to my parents. I was and will be eternally grateful to them for taking the time to escort me across the country to get the help I needed, and for their infinite love and support throughout my entire three-year ordeal.

There were about fifteen people in my building, aptly called the "Hope" building, at Menninger. As I'm always looking for signs, the fact that I was placed in the "Hope" building was very promising. The patients in our coed building were mostly women. They had all been there for quite some time when I arrived. There was a common area with couches and chairs, a TV, some tables for crafts, and a ping-pong table, which turned out to be a great activity to distract me from myself. Both sides of the main room had private, smaller classrooms. As I scanned the room, I saw people talking, laughing and hanging out together. It looked like they were... having fun. For patients in a treatment center, no one seemed to be suffering the way I was suffering. I became concerned that I wouldn't feel comfortable there, and that my dramatic meltdowns would be frowned upon. A friendly patient approached me and informed me that she would be my "buddy." Every new patient was assigned a buddy to show them the ropes. At Menninger, there was a system for everything and the expectations were high, so we all needed buddies to help guide us through the process.

There was even a system for eating. For an inpatient's first meal, for example, one did not go to the cafeteria with the rest of the group. Instead, a meal was brought to the patient, and she was expected to eat it in the little kitchenette in her community quarters. There was also a system to ensure everyone's safety. Upon arrival, all bags were checked by a staff member for possibly "dangerous" personal items, such as nail clippers, hair dryers, scissors and even dental floss. The staff member then deemed which items had to be stored in a cubby in the staff quarters, to be checked out when needed. No one was allowed to keep any sharp objects or anything with a cord in his or her room, for obvious reasons. All patients were also expected to prove that they weren't a risk to be around, by acting on their best behavior, not harming themselves or others, nor attempting to escape the facility.

Every morning the staff would take our vitals and weigh us. At the time, I had lost so much weight that I did not at all mind getting weighed. Not in the least. My svelte appearance was the ONLY positive attribute of the hell I was going through. I had never been a noticeably overweight person, but I always felt a little larger than those around me, or than I wanted to be. Now I was thiiiiiiiin, and it felt goood. After our vitals and breakfast, if we were still in the beginning levels, we were escorted to our daily classes, otherwise we could walk by ourselves at our own pace. The hospital had a point system where every point earned brought us closer to the "next level." Each higher level offered better privileges. We were given points for every class we attended. Points helped us move ahead towards our "next level," which meant more independence to walk to and from the cafeteria, to our classes and around the grounds by ourselves, without an escort.

We were given a big binder with our daily schedules and with other options for activities that we could sign up for. There was a white board that we had to sign in and out of to let the staff know where we were at all times. We were able to leave our quarters for classes, meals and to go to the gym. At first, the whole routine felt overwhelming, but over time it became no big deal to follow. I felt like hell anyway, so it didn't matter that I was confined to the hospital's guidelines, like Rupenzel to her tower. I wasn't able to enjoy doing anything out in the world, anyway.

Our daily classes focused primarily on psychology, relationships and why we turned out the way we did. They were very interesting and the teachers were extremely engaging. However, sitting through the classes all day long was highly challenging. My anxiety was through the roof, my body felt like ants were crawling all over it and the sensations of brain freeze in my head were constant. On the weekends, those at higher levels were given the opportunity to choose from a variety of off-campus field trips. The options were usually to go to a bookstore, restaurant or a movie. Even though I didn't really want to go anywhere, it felt lonely watching the majority of my co-patients leave for the day. At least when we were all together, it gave me more distraction from my situation, and I felt less fragile with my inpatient support system around.

Menninger wasn't a five-star retreat exactly, but it was a very lovely facility, especially under the circumstances. There was a hall on one side of the common area for men and a *longer* hall on the other side for women. I could not help but take note of the fact that the women's hallway was much longer and had many more rooms than the men's. Was it because this culture drives women more crazy, not supporting us for who we truly are? Or was it because women are more apt to admit when they need help, and to seek it out? Maybe it's a combination of both. Makes me wonder. My room was more than halfway down our hall. There was a charming, delicate tree outside my window, which ended up being a comfort for me during my stay. Staring at it made me feel at peace, centered and grounded. It was my steady friend.

During free time, my buddy taught me how to crochet wool hats. Even though *nothing* could fully distract me from my condition, I felt some welcomed accomplishment as I finished one hat and started another. Having been constricted by my unbearable pain for three years brought on so much self defeat, that the mere accomplishment of knitting a hat became a huge confidence boost for me. Despite my newfound hat-making hobby, my days felt long and challenging. I did my best to keep my cool, but I definitely had my fair share of breakdowns. Some were worse than others. I knew that the other patients could hear me bawling from my room, but I just couldn't help myself. I was way past the point of desperation for tranquility in my mind and body. My team of doctors, counselors and staff were phenomenal. They were beacons of light, giving me much-needed hope and support throughout my stay. There were two ladies in particular who I felt closest to, Vicki and Linda. They made me feel heard and supported, above and beyond what anyone else had throughout my journey, and were genuinely invested in my recovery. They stood by me even when I was at my weakest, encouraging me not to give up on myself. I will be forever grateful to both of those angels. They will always have a very special place in my heart.

I believe it was week four when I was finally able to go without a chaperone to the gym, dining hall, classes and elsewhere. I was even allowed to leave our quarters and walk around the beautiful courtyard on my own. I appreciated the freedom and space I was given and I took full advantage of it by spending as much time as possible outdoors. I would lie underneath a tree in the courtyard, stare at its magnificent beauty and pray, like Pocahontas to Grandmother Willow, that I would heal and live a happy life. But first, I had to get my physical symptoms under control.

One of the tests they offered at Menninger was a test that revealed which medications one's body would metabolize best. It was a tool to help figure out what would work best for each individual. The test was meant to take all the guesswork out of prescribing, thus saving time and lessening the aggravation of experimenting with multiple medications. When the test results came back, a drug cocktail was chosen for me, and I was put on it right away. During each appointment with my doctor, I would grill him about when the effects of the medication would kick in. He had to keep reminding me not to focus so intensely on exactly when the medication would work, but on the transformative healing I was receiving from my classes and from bonding with the other patients. I understood his position, but I knew that he did not fully understand mine: The buzzing, burning, spinning and inability to relax or even to sleep... I was on fire, and he expected me to just sit back patiently and read my program workbook.

Yeah, I wanted to stay focused on the program, but my burning brain had its own priorities. It wanted to know when the medicine would start working. The doctor said it could take a while to take effect. That was a bummer, but he was right about the programming at Menninger. I did learn so much about myself from all the eye-opening classes. They helped me to shift my viewpoint about myself, life and relationships, for the better. I was also given the opportunity to have conference calls with my social worker and any family members with whom I wanted to connect openly. As a young child I never wanted to hurt my parents' feelings or disappoint them in any way. It took a lot of courage to have a conversation with my dad and express my inner truths, but I am so very grateful that I did. He listened to me and shared his observations and feelings, which eased my past disappointments and allowed me to shift my perspective and move forward feeling refreshed and accepted. I love and appreciate my dad for all his love and for all he has provided me. We have created many special memories together that I will forever cherish in my heart and I look forward to many more. Even though I grew to feel renewed spiritually, I still felt trapped inside my body. My symptoms just would not let up. Thankfully, I had loving support as I awaited the effectiveness of the medication. I also gained more privileges as the weeks went by, which meant that I could receive visitors, who brought me additional comfort.

My husband had a cousin named Ilana who lived right near where I was staying. She came to visit me often and would bring me snacks. We would sit for hours and talk and cry together. She had a son who had been suffering with a traumatic mystery illness for years and she would share her concerns about him with me. I, in turn, felt safe sharing my immense suffering with her. It felt good to bond with Ilana so quickly and to have someone who supported me so deeply. Cousin Ilana shared her huge heart with me at a time when I most needed the support.

Each week at Menninger, there would be patients who were finishing up their stays and were headed home, and new patients just arriving. I was so impressed with each and every one of their courageous spirits. They all had their own challenging situations that they were determined to overcome with the help of the program. I had more respect and admiration for them than for most people I knew. It took guts to admit that they needed help, to leave the life they were familiar with, and to go to a treatment center to get that assistance. The inpatients at Menninger were down-to-earth, good people who, like me, had bigger boulders thrown on their paths than most. It was comforting to know that we were all in it together, supporting one another along the way. I was certain that the camaraderie was one of the main reasons for the high success rate at Menninger. Humans are not meant to take on life's struggles alone.

As miserable as our experiences were, being able to share about them with others, and to receive and give support, made for a very powerful healing process. We were all so vulnerable, open and raw, and thus were able to connect on a much deeper level. The only downside to the bonding was that it was hard to watch people leave. Towards the end of my program, I felt like the big kid on the block, having been there the longest. Then, the new people would reach out to me wanting my veteran support and guidance. Being the instinctive caretaker that I was, it felt good to be there for all of the new, amazing women entering the program, especially since I hadn't felt helpful to my family and friends for so long. Even though I was still suffering with my crazy symptoms, some of the new inpatients were in unbearable pain themselves and my heart went out to them.

> *"It is your decisions, and not your conditions,
> that determine your destiny."* ~Tony Robbins

SCENE 27
Accepting My Fate

Where my healing was concerned, I knew that I had given it my all. I had traveled all over the state and even across the country visiting specialists and healers, had followed countless diets and protocols and had taken boatloads of herbs, supplements and medications, and nothing had healed my condition. I'd spent a lot of the last three years feeling angry, bitter, depressed and frustrated, but I'd also spent my fair share of time learning how to feel grateful, aware and forgiving. As my time at Menninger was drawing to a close, I had to admit that I didn't get the physical healing I came for, and decided to accept whatever fate would bring.

Before I returned home, I spent much of my free time in the courtyard, doing my daily walking for exercise and lying under my Grandmother Willow tree, meditating and praying. I valued that special space that I created for myself to reflect and calm my body. At the completion of my program, I had no reprieve from my symptoms. I came to realize that my last ditch attempt at healing did not go as well as I had hoped. With a heavy heart, I started thinking about the experiences that I wished I could check off my bucket list... before I ended my life... since that seemed to be the only escape from my agony. In my condition and due to my inability to get around, I could not do many of the activities that were on my bucket list, but there was one activity in particular that I wasn't going to miss out on - SKYDIVING!

I decided that I would go home after my time at Menninger and make my skydiving dream a reality. I really had no fear of anything anymore, except for living in such excruciating pain, and I didn't care about the consequences of any possibly dangerous activities at that point. I was angry! Alongside checking off bucket list items, I also started to envision ways that I could make my exit without it being too much for my loved ones to bear. Even writing those words feels surreal from where I stand today. It's hard to believe that thinking came from within me, and yet it did.

I was days away from going home, so I made a very purposeful visit to the labyrinth in the courtyard. Walking its windy cobblestones would be my last plea to God to save me. As Lessons4Living.com describes: "A labyrinth is an ancient symbol that relates to wholeness. It combines the imagery of the circle and spiral into a meandering but purposeful path. The Labyrinth represents a journey to our own center and back again into the world. Labyrinths have long been used as mediation and prayer tools." As I slowly followed the labyrinth's path to its center, I found myself focusing on connecting to my higher power, as best I could. When I reached the end of the path in the center, I sat down on the pavement, crossed my legs, closed my eyes and began praying. I thanked God for a very meaningful and fortunate life. I thought fondly of all the different people who I had the privilege of meeting along the way. I forgave myself and others for any misunderstandings, hurts and wrongdoings that I had experienced or caused. I decided to accept my three-year hell on earth as something much bigger than I might ever understand, and I chose right then and there to look at it as part of my soul's pre-ordained journey. I thought about all of the loving relationships I had been blessed to have experienced. I let go of blaming God for not healing me.

I changed my point of view about ending my own life. I thought of the millions before me who had come to a similar crossroads and who had faced a similar defining moment - and my heart understood. While I knew that suicide left an eternal impact on loved ones who were left behind, I could no longer concern myself with anyone else. I had to put my own well-being and sanity above everyone else's, even above my own precious family. Although I knew that my actions would cause my family unspeakable pain, I realized that I had to put myself and my own needs first. I had to block out the image of the devastation that I would leave in my aftermath, and stay true to the clarity that I finally had. Besides, I knew that my family had a strong support system that would comfort them through the loss, but *I* would *not* be okay continuing to live the way I felt. I gently told God, one more time, this time without any attachment to the outcome, that I would appreciate more than anything to heal my physical trauma, and to live a long life with my family in this human form. If that destiny wasn't in the cards for me then I would do what I had to do and relieve myself of my nightmare. Shifting my viewpoint about my situation lifted a huge weight off my spirit. After that conversation with God, I truly came to be in a place of radical acceptance - devoid of anger, judgement, resentment or any further need to throw a pity-party for myself. I opened my eyes and slowly retraced my steps out of the Labyrinth.

"Fate doesn't ask you what you want.
Fate knows what's best even if you
don't." ~Nayyar Shabbir Ahmad

SCENE 28
Rebirth at Rock Bottom

"Even after the worst storms, the sun will shine again." ~Kathryn Shirley

I t was time to go home. I had watched many patients before me preparing for their exits, and at the end of their stays, they seemed to have drastically improved. Though I learned an enormous amount about myself and life during my stay at Menninger, the main symptoms that I came there to heal did not go away. They were still raging fiercely, even towards the end. I didn't know what was ahead of me, but I knew that my "last try" was nearing its end. I was going home, and I was prepared to do whatever I needed to do in order to rescue myself from the constant pain. I was also very excited to see my husband and kids. I missed them so much and couldn't wait to hold them in my arms. They were my people, my foundation, my world.

My love for my children is, to this day, the most meaningful and deepest feeling of connection I have ever felt. Giving birth and raising another human being is a life-transforming and precious experience. The connection that was created after nine months of feeling a life growing inside of me was amazing beyond description. When I finally got to hold my babies, after each birth, and watched them gaze up into my eyes, it was the most gratifying and ecstatic feeling I have ever had. My love for my three children will be forever engraved in my heart. They have brought me so much joy, insight and yes... PURPOSE! Upon returning home, it was extremely heartbreaking to look my sweet angels in the eyes, knowing that I may feel forced to permanently abandon them. That is not an experience a mother ever wants to face. I felt devastated to find myself in that situation, and hoped it wouldn't come to that.

The week after Menninger was dismal. My body still felt like it was being dragged behind a truck and I couldn't make it stop. I felt no relief from the symptoms that had been plaguing me. I told my husband that I would give the medication two more weeks to take effect, as that would be the ten-week mark, when the doctors said the meds were supposed to "kick in." In the meantime, I started to think seriously about how I would end my life in case the medication did not end up helping. I pondered how I would go about procuring a handgun for myself, as death by bullet seemed to be the quickest and most effective way out. If I did end up deciding to use the gun, I would plan to leave my husband a detailed description of how to find my body. Even though I didn't explicitly share my plan with Doron, I'm sure that my morbid conversations during that first week back home, about having reached the end of my rope, were devastating for him. In my heart, however, I knew he would understand whatever decision I chose to make.

Two weeks later, by the grace of God, I woke up on a Sunday morning and noticed my symptoms had reduced from a ten-out-of-ten to a seven! I was shocked and hopeful. I remember telling my husband that I could hang on longer living at a seven. I believe that every protocol I attempted had accumulated for my betterment and was finally paying off. Nutrition, herbal remedies, body work, stem cell treatments and other natural healing remedies can take months to kick-in and take effect. I'm sure the medication I was prescribed also contributed to relieving my ailing brain. In addition, I feel that by completely surrendering and accepting whatever was to be my fate, I was able to align with the highest version of myself, at long last.

The soul-searching, realizations and understandings that I worked so hard to embody were finally coming to fruition. I experienced a reawakening, so to speak. Everything felt like it was finally working itself out.

As I was told from the very beginning, it takes a long time for the brain to heal, and clearly that was true for me. I'd also like to believe that God, my Higher Power, was responding to my plea in the labyrinth. Whatever the case, I couldn't have been more grateful and relieved that my symptoms started to subside. I was being given another chance at life, and I felt overjoyed. I was confident that the improvement in my condition meant I would continue to heal.

> *"Remember that no matter how much it hurts right now, one day you'll look back and realize it made you stronger."* ~Unknown

SCENE 29
After the Storm

Whenever people used to speak about their transformations, rebirths, evolution and growth, I would imagine they would feel like completely new and improved versions of themselves. I pictured it like a caterpillar who had gone into her cocoon, through chrysalis, and had come out transformed into a totally different creature - a beautiful butterfly. I imagined that such a transformative experience would make me feel like an entirely reinvented being. Well, that's not exactly how it works, folks. Or at least that's not how it worked for me. A butterfly, after all, is still a caterpillar between those two wings. It's a caterpillar with an upgrade. I have not become a completely different person, as I once thought I would after such an experience. I am still that caterpillar between my newfound wings, I just don't let the fear and sadness rule me anymore, so I feel more joyful, more free and more *me*.

A huge part of my growth was the radical acceptance of myself, in my entirety. I've clearly been through the ringer and then some, but during my time of such intense struggle, I experienced a deep evolution of myself... I grew wings. And I love the better version of me that I worked so hard to rediscover and set free. I grew to such a place where I was finally living at a higher vibrational level of existence, on the "high flying disc," as Abraham Hicks would call it.

There once were aspects of myself that I did not accept, such as deep-seated fear, sadness and insecurity, which festered inside of me all the time, and which, as a young girl, I remember expressing in fits of tears… by myself… alone in my room. I believed then that it was unacceptable to have those less-than-happy feelings. From all the soul searching I did during my three years in agony, I came to accept *all* of my emotions and to know how important it is to feel and express them, the good, the bad, the ugly and everything in between. In doing so, I have given voice to that young, timid, little girl who was silenced so long ago. My tragedy pushed me to finally undertake a dynamic healing process for my inner child. Because I was never listening to my inner voice or the voice of The Universe, I believe that I had to experience the devastating physical brain injuries in order to make me stop, look within and work on myself.

Through my inner-work, I learned not to negate my more lamentable emotions, but rather to accept them when they do rear their heads. Those parts of us will always be there, but they will appear less and less often when we allow them to come forward without resistance. As Universal Law states, a message that we are supposed to hear will keep getting louder and louder until we hear it, understand it and act upon it. To save yourself years of agony, I highly recommend listening to the guidance that The Universe is giving you! We must recognize there is no such thing as *perfect* the way we like to define it in our world. And quite frankly, we would be bored and unstimulated if there were. Our job is not to seek perfection, but rather to love ALL of who we are, as perfectly-imperfect, divine beings. Nature is the best teacher of this. The soothing, calm seas can turn into rough waters and devastating tsunamis. The beautiful roses have sharp thorns. The bees who make our world bloom and create the sweetest honey can sting. We actually are "perfect," just like nature - tumult, thorns, stingers, warts and all.

Being aware of our inner dialogue is truly what creates the types of experiences we will have. As 'they' say, "What you think about, you bring about." If nothing else, my journey has taught me to change the way I communicate with myself. I have learned that becoming friends with every aspect of me, starting with the messages between my own two ears, is the road to happiness. Now, on a daily basis, I practice my engrained affirmations like, "I am healthy, I am happy, I am living my purpose." I laugh more, at myself and at life. Even as I began writing the memories down from the three years of hell I experienced, I realized they came from a place of higher awareness. I was writing with a deeper sense of self and a clearer perspective after I had emerged from the dark tunnel. The "healed me" wrote about the "wounded me" with such empathy and compassion. From my new vantage point, I could better understand why I had to walk along the path I did, to become who I am today.

When we learn how to shift our perspectives on how we view ourselves and others, we will come to understand life in all of its glorious polarity. Polarity is a hard reality for most of us here on the earth plane to wrap our noggins around. Sometimes we have to go through - and/or watch those we love go through - challenging times, in order to find what we are seeking. Sometimes we have to experience unsatisfying situations in order to be able to identify the satisfying ones. As Abraham Hicks reminds us, "When you know what you don't like, you know what you do like." What we don't like will inevitably guide us to what we do like. Having the strength and courage to push through *whatever* is sent our way, even the disastrous, will bring feelings of empowerment and elation, which is what we all desire. We may view negative occurrences as tragedies because they are unpleasant, but I believe those experiences are brought to us for reasons beyond our limited human comprehension. Having trust and faith will help us stay strong and positive so that we can continue along our journey towards happiness and to our ultimate purposes.

As I wrap *My Wake Up Fall,* my purpose has never been more clear. I am meant to set my caged self free to fly and to help others to do the same. I feel light, exhilarated and grateful for my life, for everything I have experienced and for the wonderful people in it. I am thrilled to continue putting the pieces of my life's puzzle together even further, and I look forward to unveiling more self discoveries and insights. The path of self discovery is never complete. Stay present and enjoy the journey.

....

"You can never meet your potential until you truly learn to love yourself." ~Teresa Collins

....

SCENE 30
New York State of Intuition (Epilogue)

By June of 2019, I was feeling better than I had felt in five years. I had been feeling very well for the past two years, even though I wasn't completely recovered. I still experienced fatigue and fogginess, but I was grateful to be able to participate in my own life again. Overall, I was doing well… except when I found myself steeped in a bath of chemicals!

I had been extremely sensitive to smells and lights when I was at my worst, so much that it would completely set me off when my kids would spray perfume or use paints or other chemicals in the house. I assumed they should *know* not to use toxins, especially with me being in such a sensitive state, and I would become panicky when they did, which would further infuriate me and exacerbate my discomfort. Then, I'd have no choice but to wait for my overwhelming, fight-or-flight sensations to pass. I felt helpless against the inevitable reaction I would experience. Now, two years later, I am very careful about what products my family and I use. I am also careful to move away from chemicals the moment I sense them around, which works… when I actually listen to my intuition. But vanity sometimes gets the best of me.

I planned a fun trip to New York with my dear friend, Heather, for our fiftieth birthdays. I decided to get my hair blown out the day before we were scheduled to leave. A girl's always got to be happy with her hair! Immediately upon entering the salon, I noticed a very strong chemical odor. I could hear a voice in my head screaming, "LEAVE NOW!" At that point in my life, I was very good at listening to that voice. Unfortunately, there was an equally loud (vain) voice rationalizing why I should tough it out in the chemical bath. So, I sat and waited for my turn. I suppose I felt overly confident, since I had been doing so well, that I'd be able to handle the overwhelming odors. After all, the products weren't even being used on me, they were just in the air. How bad could it really get?

That evening, I started feeling my frontal lobe tightening up, and felt a horribly familiar sensation that I always despised - a throbbing that started making its way through my head. I was kicking myself for not listening to my inner voice the minute I smelled the chemicals. Here I was, the day before a big trip, and I was too stubborn to leave the salon. It was one of those moments where I wished that I could just turn back time and take a re-do, but I couldn't. The next morning, I was still feeling unstable, but I thought I would be OK, so I grabbed my bags and headed out on our adventure. While Heather and I were sitting in the airport waiting to board the plane, reality hit. The sensations were progressing quickly. I was feeling anxious and questioning whether I should even go to New York. I decided to push through my symptoms and concerns about them worsening. I bucked up and boarded the plane.

During the flight, my symptoms continued to worsen. I became very triggered and started fearing that my nightmare was about to begin all over again. My confidence was fading, as fear and helplessness crept in. Were my three years of hell repeating themselves all over again? I shrank with despair at the mere thought of it. The tears began welling up in my eyes, and I started to cry as I felt the terrifying symptoms worsening. My emotions were hard to control, like in the past, and I was scared. I could only imagine what was going through the minds of the two men I was sandwiched between on the plane, as tears streamed down my face. At that moment, I just wanted my husband by my side to console me. Stifling my sobs through the flight, I somehow found my strength and survived the trip to New York.

It has been said that crying is a purifying balm for the soul. My soul must be *very* pure by now. The following morning, after my first night in the hotel, by the grace of God, I felt much better than I had anticipated I would feel. Heather and I ended up having a lot of fun in New York, but it really got me thinking about how quickly I could go from zero to sixty - from feeling stable and peaceful to feeling like I was falling back down into a very dark abyss. I didn't like the forty eight hours of discomfort after my salon experience, but it served as an important reminder to be grateful for each "normal" day and not to take anything in life for granted. It also showed me that being extra cautious for the sake of my well-being was beyond necessary, so that I didn't regress. I was reminded, with that experience, to be patient with myself when I felt thrown back into rough waters. No few-day irritation from chemical exposure was going to derail me from my progress towards optimal health and well-being. It was just a small set back, not a major regression. After all, sometimes, like a bow, we have to pull back in order to shoot forward. I'm getting more confident in the archery of my life.

· ·

"My dark days made me strong. Or maybe
I already was strong, and the dark days
made me prove it." ~Emery Lord

· ·

LESSON 1
Listen to the Universe

....

"The Universe is always speaking to us through little messages, coincidences and synchronicities that remind us to stop, look around and be present." ~Unknown

....

I truly believe The Universe is sending signs and messages to each and every one of us, at all times, helping to guide us towards our best paths, and giving us the exact guidance that we need at the perfect times. I started recognizing those signs and messages from The Universe as soon as I learned that It was speaking to me. I would even receive answers to questions that were haunting me, through quotes people would send me, the podcasts I would "randomly" choose to listen to, and through songs that I would hear on the radio. I came to recognize certain symbols as my own, unique totems of hope, such as rainbows, hearts and numbers.

I also truly believe there are many of us who miss that Divine guidance, day in and day out. I definitely used to be one of those people. I have heard many times from my mentors that the more we ignore our messages from The Universe, the louder the messages will get, and they don't always come in the most desirable of ways. I think that at some level, my fall was The Universe telling me to WAKE UP and LISTEN! I mean, it was my *fourth* head injury! And it got my undivided attention for three straight years. Actually, you could say that I spent that entire time period learning to decipher The Universe's tongue.

We all have a special and unique purpose in this life, and it's our job to listen to our inner guidance to figure that out, and to live as the best, most authentic versions of ourselves. Taking the time to slow down and to have an awareness of the present moment will help you to hear the whispers of The Universe and the messages that are meant for you to hear. In this fast-paced world, in which we put so much pressure on ourselves to *do it all*, it's so important to take some time for yourself each day to get quiet, go within, reflect on your path and upon how you are feeling. The guidance you will receive from that place will be much more profound than any that comes from your ego mind. And if you feel misguided or rejected at any point, remember the old adages, "Rejection is God's protection" and "Rejection is redirection."

Don't ignore that "knowing voice," that inner guidance inside of you, when making decisions, or ever! That is The Universe communicating with you. Once you become aligned with the higher energies of the world, you will become happier and your life will flow much more easily. Let The Universe work magic through you, and watch your life improve in leaps and bounds.

· ·

*"Our life does not always turn out the
way we planned, but sometimes that's
because what we planned wasn't supposed
to be our life."* ~Parna Nandi

· ·

LESSON 2
Judging

JUDGEMENTAL

You cannot know what another goes through,
Until you have had the same experience, too.
It's not fair to judge from where you sit,
You couldn't possibly understand this deep, dark pit.
Unless you've experienced PTSD,
You can't understand the fear inside me.
As time goes by and I can't see the light,
My body fatigues keeping up with the fight.
The symptoms and sensations, when will they break?
The longer they last, the harder to take.
I continue to think in my optimistic way,
And pray that I'll meet my freedom day.

••

*"When you judge another, you do not
define them, you define yourself as someone
who needs to judge." ~Wayne Dyer*

••

Humans judge! It's in our DNA. And then we judge the fact that we are judging. Even whoever wrote the Torah knew this. In the Torah it commands us to, "Judge favorably," meaning that the author knew that we humans were going to judge, so God challenged us to do so favorably. Let's face it, judging others is going to happen, but until you have experienced what another person has gone through, there is really no way you can possibly relate to their exact situation. Therefore, your opinions are nothing more than assumptions. As my dad always said, opinions are like assholes... everybody's got one.

It is a waste of time and energy to focus our attention on what others are doing, especially when it's coming from a negative perspective. Practice catching yourself in the act when you are having negative judgements and redirect your thoughts to something more constructive and positive. One powerful technique I learned from a very rewarding, year-long DBT (Dialectical Behavioral Therapy) course I took was to follow the rule of "STOP!" Whenever I have an awareness of any negative thinking that doesn't serve me, I say "STOP!" firmly to myself, and refocus. I redirect and encourage myself to think about topics that make me feel happy, to replace the negative thoughts. The more I practice the STOP exercise, the less often those negative thoughts arise. This practice has been extremely helpful for me.

Having an awareness of the fact that you are judging is the first step in creating new, more positive neural pathways. We are all on our own journeys, finding our own ways, and still we are all in this together, meant to support one another, side by side, not to judge each other. We are meant to learn and grow from our "mistakes," so be a friend to yourself when things aren't going the way you'd like them to go, don't judge yourself so harshly when they don't work out. Be kind to yourself and don't set yourself up for failure and disappointment by creating assumptions and judgments that might not be true and which are certainly not productive. A positive and determined attitude will bring goodness into your life over time. Be patient, open and allowing of all that The Universe has to offer.

> "Before you assume, learn the facts.
> Before you judge, understand why.
> Before you hurt someone, feel.
> Before you speak, think." ~Evana Valle

LESSON 3
Forgiveness

This is a big one. Forgiveness of yourself, others and God. Dr. Dave, one of my favorite mentors during my three rough years, told me to always remember to stay in forgiveness and repeat over and over, "I forgive myself, I forgive others, I forgive God." This mantra has been very beneficial to me since I started using it. It is true that we can be our own worst critics. We can be so loving and comforting to our friends and family when they make mistakes or lose out on something. Why is it that we break *ourselves* down when we experience challenging times? Forgiving yourself takes the pressure off, giving you permission to make mistakes, while keeping your confidence strong. It's not a matter of *if* we are going to make mistakes, have failures or lose out, it's a matter of *when*. Flubbing up will happen at times; it's just part of being human. What is important is that we learn from those moments and have compassion for ourselves in the process.

Forgiving others can be a tough one, too. No one likes the feeling of being wronged by another. It hurts our ego and our feelings to be treated unkindly. In some situations you may be able to forgive another over time and still maintain a relationship with them. There are also the types of betrayal and loss which make it just too painful to tolerate being around the person who we feel wronged us. In these cases, I'm not saying you should forget the person's actions. However, when you are able to make peace and forgive your perpetrator, you will inevitably set yourself free from the toxicity of holding onto anger or hate. Forgiveness allows you to walk away peacefully, which will have a positive impact on your life. You will radiate an energy that will attract goodness into your existence. It takes practice, but it works.

Forgiving God is another difficult challenge, especially for those who are fatally ill or have lost children, parents or loved ones in tragic situations. The pain and helplessness we feel when we think God has not responded to our prayers is extremely difficult to endure or comprehend. We are left feeling unworthy, extremely bitter and full of rage. During my three-year odyssey, I spent many hours yelling and screaming at God, feeling ignored and unimportant. It wasn't until I started practicing forgiveness that I found the peace I'd been searching for. When we can surrender, let go of control, and stop resisting life's plan for us, we will then create a space for what we desire to come true.

Forgiveness doesn't mean you excuse any crime that you feel was committed against you; it just means you excuse yourself from being the victim. Holding a grudge makes you weak; forgiving sets you free. When you forgive yourself and others, you will release yourself from the prison of the past and from any residual anger that may be lingering with it. After all, it has been said that for-*give*-ness is a gift you *give* yourself by releasing the heavy feelings of resentment. Give forgiveness a try and see what happens.

....

> *"In the blink of an eye everything can change. So*
> *forgive often and love with all your heart. You*
> *may not have that chance again."* ~Zig Ziglar

....

LESSON 4
You Do You

"The one thing that you have that nobody else has is YOU. Your voice, your mind, your story, your vision. So write and draw and build and play and dance and live only as you can." ~Neil Gaiman

I n the immortal words of Dr. Seuss, "Why fit in when you were born to stand out?"

When we are young and wanting to fit in, make friends and be accepted by others, it is very common for us to exaggerate who we really are and where our true interests lie. This may not be true for everyone, though I think a large majority of us can relate. We all want to be liked, and sometimes we think that if we hide our truth and say what we think others want to hear, we will gain their affection and approval. Lord knows I spent my fair share of time acting that way. I was always trying to be a people-pleaser and to be liked by my friends. Let me be the first to tell you how exhausting and unrewarding that was. My mom even used to call me "The Clone" of my best friend from elementary school, because she observed that I imitated my friend's every expression and her demeanor. I even grew to have her same interests. I so desperately wanted to be liked and accepted that I went along with whatever my friends did and became who I thought they wanted me to be, at my own expense. After my three-year trauma, I was finally able to let go of that act, which was a habit that I had formed so long ago, and reveal my true colors. My pain forced me to get to know my real self, and *that* was freeing and rewarding.

If we continue to try too hard to please others, over time we are likely to lose awareness of who we really are and may start to feel unsatisfied and lost. Stop people-pleasing! Don't sell yourself short. We must find a way to be true to our God-given uniqueness! If we were all the same, life would be so boring. Set yourself free by getting to know the true you and what makes you happy. Living authentically will take a big weight off your back, and will add a pep to your step. I say this from experience, and I truly love the "me" that I have freed from the facade.

Figuring out our place in the world can be so rewarding. The Universe will do its best to get our attention and guide us toward our purpose, sometimes even with blows to the head. We must listen carefully in order to hear the guidance that The Universe is constantly whispering. Nurturing our relationship with ourselves and our Higher Power through meditation, prayer and other self-empowering exercises will help us to cultivate the best versions of ourselves. My daily rituals will differ from yours. The whole point here is to find what makes your soul sing and dance. You get to co-create your own path with God. The magic is in the journey, in getting to figure out the practices that bring *you* to life. Cheers to you in your soul searching! I'm so excited for you to meet this special version of yourself.

And, remember to put yourself first. You are no good to anyone else if you aren't healthy and happy, yourself. You do you! You are meant to be here pursuing your purpose and enjoying your life in your own unique way. Put on your own oxygen mask, fill your own cup and wipe your own tush first, my friends!

....

"Today you are you. That is truer than true. There is no one alive who is you-er than YOU." ~Dr. Seuss

....

LESSON 5
Accept Everyone's Own Path

"You might be walking on the same road of life with your friends but remember that everyone has a unique journey." ~Annah Maponya

Have you ever wanted another person to "wake up" to something that was negatively affecting their lives? Or has someone tried desperately to get you to see something that you were not ready to see? Many of us find it easy to dole out great advice to others about how they "should" be living their lives, but cannot seem to apply that same advice to ourselves. I know I've been guilty of this behavior. There were many times when I tried to open certain friends' eyes to damaging situations they were in, but I had blinders on when it came to my own life. Whenever anyone would give me advice or share what they had been observing in some of *my* relationships, I would become very defensive and reject their input. I guess the old saying is true: love (or lust or codependency or whatever it is)... is indeed blind. I had to experience those relationships for my own growth, though. Nothing anyone said could have altered my path. I have come to understand that trying to change anyone's trajectory might actually interfere with their growth, though planting seeds *is* fair game. I highly recommend sprinkling kernels of wisdom. I enjoy being a spiritual gardener, myself.

Sometimes we have to bring someone to our vista in order for them to see something they couldn't see from where they were standing. Imagine being in a national park with various viewpoints from which to look out at the glory of nature. You and your friends are all standing at different overlooks. One of your friends says he can only see a barren field from his position. You are standing at a point where you can see beyond his limited view, all of the gorgeous wildflowers, butterflies, waterfalls, rainbows… and maybe even a unicorn if you look deeply enough into the valley! You encourage him to come over to your vantage point so he can see what you are seeing - what was always there the entire time, but simply not visible from where he was standing. Sometimes we just need to invite others to our viewpoints, and be open to having them lead us to theirs. When we live openly, we will inevitably see and learn something that we could not see or comprehend from where we stood. We are, after all, each other's teachers.

Even with my husband, I used to set myself up for disappointment and aggravation, constantly expecting him to be able to see what I was seeing from my point of view, when we were standing at different vistas. I used to put a lot of energy into questioning why he did this or didn't do that, to a point that I started experiencing a lot of stress and frustration because of his choices. I finally figured out that I could make my own choices about how I reacted to him. I learned how to allow him the space to be himself and started focusing my energy on supporting him along his path, rather than on judging him as someone who was experiencing life from a "barren field" vantage point. When we see our partners as ogres, that's who we'll get! Luckily, I came to a new understanding of my husband, and I now see him as my prince… most of the time. There are so many wonderful things I love about Doron, and it is much more rewarding to focus on those things rather than on all of my old expectations about who he *should* be.

When we stop interfering with other people's paths, and stop trying to change them, our relationships will flourish. We all need to learn our own lessons in our own ways. We're not meant to "play God" in others' plays. When we release the need to interfere along another's path, that will also be freeing for us. Then we won't have the self-imposed burden of controlling anyone else. Anyone who is a parent can relate, I'm sure. It's damn challenging to be the boss of littles all the time. And, let's face it, when we focus on other people, it is merely a distraction from focusing on our own self discovery, which is where our attention should be kept. Focusing on ourselves is plenty to deal with as it is. Let others live out their own destinies in their own time and in the way that they need to, for their own growth. Accepting everyone's own path is a lesson that takes *a lot* of practice. I still catch myself slipping up at times with this teaching; though as I continue along my journey, I embrace the challenge of allowing everyone to be where they are, and to grow at their own pace.

· ·

"No one changes unless they want to. Not if
you beg them. Not if you shame them. Not if
you use reason, emotion, or tough love. There's
only one thing that makes someone change:
their own realization that they need to do it.
And there's only one time it will happen: when
they decide they're ready." ~Lori Deschene

· ·

LESSON 6
On Relationships

As we know, supporting others means allowing them to find themselves in their own time. So often when we join with another person in a love relationship, there is an expectation that it is our partner's job to make us happy. In the beginning, it's easy to envision people the way we want them to be (doting, always complimentary... and growing more successful by the day, for example), and then we become disappointed when they don't follow our script. We all have different ideas about how to give and receive love. No one way is right or wrong, better or worse. The key is to be able to identify the ways in which you and your partner give and receive love and to communicate effectively when you need something different. For more information about this concept read the book "The Five Love Languages: How to Express Heartfelt Commitment to Your Mate" by Gary Chapman. It is a wonderful resource.

Expectations and scripts don't work. They set the other person up for failure every time, and they set us up to feel let down. When we can accept our partners for who they truly are, pros and cons, we can then allow them the space they need to grow, and work on their own contentment. Their happiness is their responsibility and our happiness is ours - and only ours. Happiness comes from within. Happiness comes when we learn to put ourselves first and love and accept ourselves exactly as we are.

As the sages have taught, we can only evolve to the next level of ourselves when we come to accept and unconditionally love our current state of being. We can support one another, but there is no amount of money or attention from another being that can make us whole and complete. We are on our own individual journeys, and our most important task in life is to find our own peace and joy; only then can we truly enjoy life with others. Besides, it would be quite lonely and boring without others in the mix! Having said that, I do believe that relationships must have boundaries that consist of respect, empathy and good communication. Flowers and foot rubs don't hurt either. When two people come together, it is important to remember they have been raised with different parenting styles, have experienced the world differently, and have their own individual personalities, as well. When we don't consider these factors, our expectations can get in the way and can make relating to one another much harder than necessary.

My marriage is a perfect example of two diverse worlds coming together, to co-create our shared existence. My husband was born and raised in South Africa through the age of fourteen, while I was born in the USA. The two cultures are very different, as were our individual upbringings. In South Africa, his life centered around family and community over individual pursuits. His parents are still married, while mine are divorced. He was surrounded by a large, extended family almost every weekend, while my extended family only saw each other for special occasions. While my husband and I agree on many aspects regarding how we live our lives and view the world, there are some ideas that we disagree on due to our unique backgrounds. With regard to parenting, for example, because Doron was more grounded in who he was, he trusted that being strict would help guide our kids to become the best versions of themselves, and he was not concerned whatsoever about them feeling unloved when he would be stern with them. I, on the other hand, was not as confident in myself, so I tredded more softly in my parenting style, hoping to protect them from feeling any type of rejection. The first step in making a relationship work is to respect one another and accept and acknowledge our differences. No matter what the situation, only when we accept each other for *all* that we are, can we build a functional and enjoyable relationship. Our different circumstances shaped each of us into who we are. No experiences were better or worse, they were simply different. My husband and I continue to choose to unite as a team and work through the challenges that arise from our diverse backgrounds.

Our partners can't play every role or fulfill every need in our lives. Making time for other relationships outside of our romantic relationships is also important. It goes without saying that the relationship with ourselves must be constantly developed. Friendships must be cultivated, too! Friends play important roles in our lives. Some friends are there to spill our guts to, others make us laugh and some are just easy to be around. Friendships teach us so much about life. They teach us how to interact, forgive, laugh and challenge ourselves. Friends support us when we are down and rejoice in our celebrations. It's important to have boundaries in all relationships, of course. Being open and clear about your comfort level with your friends helps keep things pleasant and peaceful. Trying to please your friends all the time isn't healthy for either of you. (Refer back to Lesson 4 if you haven't already grasped this). Let your friends know when you are able to show up for them and when you aren't, without feeling guilty. And be prepared to accept the same from them, without judging their "lack of support." There are always two sides to every story, and both my friends and I did a lot of jumping to conclusions without investigating the other side, which was not fair to any of us. After all, as it has been said, making ASSumptions makes an "ASS" out of "U" and me.

Jumping to conclusions can leave us with ideas and feelings that may not even be the truth. That is something I came to learn first-hand through my ordeal. Needless to say, everything I went through helped me grow and gain a deeper appreciation for all the relationships in my life, even the unexpected ones. The all-knowing Universe sent me the exact people I needed at the exact right time, which was a saving grace, especially since some of my friends couldn't be there for me. It was all as it was supposed to be. Only when I didn't have many people to turn to, did I learn that I had to rely on myself first and foremost. I grew to learn how to be there for myself and to transform the dialogue within to become more positive and encouraging, so that I could always go there for support. We must nurture the relationship with ourselves. We all need to become our own best friends, partners and parents.

Now, after all I've been through, I can honestly say that I am happy with my most important relationship - the one with myself. It continues to evolve and become more and more satisfying every day, as I put these lessons into practice. Remembering to laugh with and at myself makes the journey all that much more enjoyable. My experience during those three years enabled me to truly understand and improve my own reactions to, and relationships with, others. It also taught me the importance of assessing situations from a more objective and compassionate perspective. I'm still working on mastering that. If only my darn ego wouldn't get in my way!

> *"You cannot be lonely if you like the person you're alone with."* ~Wayne Dyer

LESSON 7
Be Open to New Perspectives

We can only see the view from where we stand, but that doesn't mean that what we see is all that exists. Have you ever felt so certain about something, only to get more information that helps you to see it in a new light and come to a different conclusion? That happens all the time, folks. We don't know what we don't know! We believe what we want to believe, based on what makes sense from our current vantage point. However, when we look at life from a different angle, our outlook can evolve. Sometimes we need to walk around the mountain to get a fresh view, one with less clouds and more visibility. Only then can we comprehend the subject from a different perspective, and gain a more enlightened awareness.

Another issue that can arise with regard to perspective is accepting another's opinion as fact before we have had the opportunity to investigate anything for ourselves. I'm sure you've had a friend share their opinion about another person, a restaurant, a movie, a book, etc., and then you find yourself taking on that perspective before ever even experiencing those elements for yourself. We are quickly convinced by another's opinion, which is merely that, *an opinion*. Wouldn't you rather be your own judge? The fun in exploring life is being able to come to your own conclusions. It is OK to be different from other people. It is OK to agree to disagree. It is OK to be authentically *you*.

You were meant to be *you*! You are the only one who can be, after all! The world wants to know you, hear your opinions and learn what you have to share. Sharing your story and perspective can help others learn about themselves, too. Learning to converse with another without having any emotional attachment to their perspective is the challenge at hand. Having discourse with another person who is on a different side of the fence from you isn't always about striving to be right; rather, it's about being open to seeing another's viewpoint. It's when we preach and judge that chaos ensues. Stay open-minded and accepting, and give others the space to be themselves and to have their own perspectives. Then your interactions will be pleasant and enjoyable.

"The real voyage of discovery consists not in seeking new landscapes, but in having new eyes." ~Marcel Proust

LESSON 8
Living with Love

T hroughout my exploration in self healing, I became aware of a common theme that was always the same no matter what the source: love is the answer to everything. Living our lives in a state of love rather than fear is a requirement for happiness, one which will enable us to align with our source energy. I remember experiencing many uplifting moments in my childhood when my body felt a wave of exhilaration flowing through it. I didn't understand what that magical feeling was back then, but I am very aware of it's meaning now: I was experiencing pure love.

As I continue to keep my mind, body and soul connected and in a state of love through positive thinking, meditation, communing with nature, healthy eating and exercising, I am able to bring about that same childhood wave of delight more often. Love is my natural state and the place in which I choose to reside. Love is where I am my most authentic self. Love is where I have no inhibitions or judgements. Love is where I experience the most joy and contagious giggling. When we are in a state of fear, the antithesis of love, we are in a state of resistance, which keeps us from achieving our most desired dreams. Ask yourself, what brings you the most joy in life? When do you feel most fulfilled? When do you feel the most grounded and grateful? Listen to the answers to those questions, and you will be living in love.

• •

"Love is the answer that everyone seeks...
love is the language that every heart
speaks." ~Helen Steiner Rice

• •

MY CREW

I want to take some time here to thank those who played any role in my crazy three-year journey. From where I stand today, I have a much better understanding about the people who The Universe chose to bring forward during my time of need. The people who show up for us are not necessarily going to be our best friends or even our immediate or extended family, and that's OK.

No matter how you showed up for me, even if it was by sending me positive thoughts and prayers, I am extremely grateful. There are some who I want to recognize as the key players, a cast of characters who were exactly the angels I needed to help me through my trauma.

Many people came into my world at precisely the right time, and I will be forever grateful to each and every one of them. They accepted me, supported me, nurtured me, guided me and loved me. Their time and concern meant more than words can ever express. I wish I could write a whole scene about each one of them, but there are too many. How blessed am I?

To my crew, each of you will be forever in my thoughts and in my heart. I plan to pay it forward and to show my thankfulness for how you showed up for me by supporting others who are experiencing trauma the way you all supported me through mine. Sending untold gratitude to: my six parents, my sisters - Yael Kantor and

Issy Kleiman, Kelly Hudson, Abby Lodmer, Michelle Romaro, Susan Moini, Heidi Koss, Dr. Blye, Dr. Steven Hall, Dr. Jeannette Birnbach, Dr. Kurt, Heather Taylor, Ana Proctor, Connie Sadis, Dr. Dawn April, Jadzia Torres, Hippocrates staff, Marc Lainhart, Dr. Rachel Catini, Dr. Merrill, Dr. Yardley and staff, Dr. Kim Kelly, Dr. Amy Wells, and my whole team at Menninger, especially Vicki and Linda.

This book would not be half as legible as it is without the editing expertise of my main editor, Abby Lodmer, in addition to the priceless editing support and creative suggestions from three other special women - Connie Sadis, Stephanie Lecovin and Tori Maidenberg.

And of course, I could not have made it through my dreadful situation without my loving husband, Doron. I recall a time when Doron and I were lying in bed and I was having thoughts of ending my life. I was caressing his face, gazing into his eyes and feeling grateful for the love that we had shared. I didn't say anything, but he could read my mind. He began to tear up and said to me, "Why does it feel like you are saying goodbye to me? I don't want to do this without you, I need you in my life!" His words broke my heart, and so I chose to continue the fight. Besides having the motherly instinct to continue to endure my dreadful situation for the sake of my children, Doron was my other reason for living, my rock and my biggest supporter. I want to thank you, Doron, from the bottom of my heart, for loving me and believing in me even when you thought that it was too much for you to take. Your patience was beyond astonishing. I appreciate you letting me curl up in your lap thousands of times and melt into your nurturing embrace. You showed me what true love really is.

To my children, Sammy, Nate and Kennedy: it is very difficult for children to watch their mother struggle. All three of you were able to dig deep within and handle our experience with strength, courage, compassion and humor. You were strong for me when I had no more strength for myself. You were courageous for me when I felt defeated. You were hilarious for me when I needed a spark of joy. You were comforting to me when I was in distress. You clearly are my earth angels, and I know that without you I couldn't have pushed through. No other beings will ever know the depth of my love. As my children, you are the only ones who know the sound of my heart from the inside. Thank you for your unconditional and contagious love!

RESOURCES

Inspiring Songs:

Good to be Alive - Andy Grammer
Inspired me to keep pushing through. It reminded me that life is an amazing gift, and while it entails times of struggle, it is also full of joy and happiness, too. This song gave me determination to get myself to a comfortable place.

Bright - Echosmith
This song helped me by connecting my thoughts with the magnificent Universe and Spirit. It helped me realize there is so much more I don't understand, but the Universe has my back and will ultimately guide me to my best path.

So Alive - The Goo Goo Dolls
Another inspiring song to motivate me to never give up on myself, no matter how challenging a situation. The beat got me excited to be well again.

I Lived - One Republic
Reminded me to live life to the fullest- to get everything out of the struggles and celebrate. Never live in fear.

Something in the Water - Carrie Underwood
This song was recommended to me by my wise and gifted chiropractor, Dr. Dave Merrill. The music is set at a high frequency, which can actually help in healing the body. The lyrics connected me to Spirit, angels and to all of the entities that exist, which we cannot see with

our plain eyes. It helped me hold on to the hope that I would indeed heal.

Just Be Held - Casting Crowns

This is a beautiful song that my loving third caretaker Michelle introduced to me. It taught me to trust in God and to be willing to stop holding on so tightly, to let go and know that God is there for us, always, no matter what the outcome. We are an everlasting consciousness. We must stop living in fear.

The Fight Song - Rachel Platten

This song reminded me of how strong I am. It gave me the courage to keep on moving through the nightmare I found myself in. It helped me find *me*. It guided me to connect with and to love myself unconditionally.

Drive - Incubus (Brandon Boyd)

This amazing song reminded me not to be led by fear, but to instead take the wheel and drive myself on my own path. Too often, fear creeps in and gets the best of us, but we always have the choice to take charge and to choose love.

JOURNALING

One of the classes I participated in during my stay at Hippocrates Health Institute was a journaling class. Journaling had been recommended to me many times in the past as a therapeutic activity for releasing my pain and upsets. I was always a bit nervous to write down my most private feelings in a book, knowing that someone might read it without my permission, so I never started. The journaling class reinforced the benefits of putting my feelings down on paper, as a very constructive process for healing. One day, we were asked to answer some questions and write letters to loved ones about past hurts, and I immediately experienced relief and fulfillment after sharing my words with the whole class. I highly recommend giving therapeutic letter writing and journaling a try for yourself. There are many different ways to journal, so explore your options. I have included a list of questions below, which you can pick from to get you started. Pick a number in your head, then go to that number below and write out your immediate response to the question without thinking too much about it. Let yourself dream BIG, and have fun with it. Just start writing. You'll be amazed. I have also shared my responses to four questions below, as examples. It is gratifying to look back at those journal entries, five years after they were written, to see how far I've come and how much I have aligned with my manifestations.

Questions from the Hippocrates Health Institute journaling class, which I randomly chose:

1. If my soul could speak it would say...

Joelle, you are a very beautiful, loving person, full of bright light and healthy energy. You are hiding it and creating discomfort for yourself. You need to LET GO NOW and trust that The Universe has your back and your best interest at heart. You have so much to celebrate, enjoy and so much to live for. PLEASE START NOW and it will all come to you as planned. Enjoy each moment. Cherish your gifts. Celebrate yourself and those you love so deeply. Nothing is as earth-shattering or serious as you think it is. Laugh as much as you can. Let go of others' opinions. Set yourself free and shine, shine, shine for the world and mostly for yourself! You are truly a gift to The Universe and you are so very loved. Cheers to this wonderful, rewarding experience. LOVE LOVE LOVE!

2. When I look at the world outside myself I see...

I see that I'm not as good or successful as others. My life doesn't seem as exciting or fulfilling as the lives of others. I want to be doing more and accomplishing tasks and goals that boost my self-esteem and image. I feel "less than" and "not enough." Feeling this way brings me down and causes me to carry around a heavy, sad feeling most of the time. I also see that I can choose to change my life. I AM enough and I CAN accomplish any task or goal I set for myself. I can redefine how I see myself, without complaining or putting myself down. I am putting myself first now. I will be patient and kind as I follow my new path.

3. People expect me to be...

People expect me to be available, to follow through, to be on time, be nice, be understanding and gentle, be perfect, do whatever they want, see life their way, not talk back, be quiet, be better, listen, deal with it and believe whatever they say. These expectations weigh me down and overwhelm me. I don't want to have those expectations put on me any longer. Living with them puts too much pressure on me, and I disappoint myself when I cannot follow through. I LET GO of all those demands and put ME first. Moving forward, I will do as I see fit for myself in each situation, and I will not worry if others don't approve. I AM in charge of my journey.

4. I can afford to be wrong about...

I can afford to be wrong about the story I created regarding the way I view myself and others. I have done so much soul searching due to my injury and symptoms, and I have come to realize that I have not been serving myself or my relationships in a positive manner. Being hard on myself only makes me feel worse. When I can be kind to myself first, then my relationships, career and other important aspects of my life will fall into place. I can afford to let go of my past patterns and thinking, and to try something completely new. I love my life and the people in it. I enjoy feeling joy, happiness, love and laughter. I want to exercise, eat healthy, spend time with friends, go to the movies and experience all the wonderful moments life has to offer. I am done suffering, and I choose to move forward and improve my life. My symptoms will disappear very soon. I will continue to sleep well and heal well. I am so thankful for this opportunity.

JOURNALING

KEY PRINCIPLES

The art and heart of reflection by Stephanie Dowrick

1. Your life is a work in progress. So is your journal.
2. Write your journal for yourself, not for anyone else.
3. Keep your journals in a safe place. You will write most freely when your journals remain in private.
4. Journal writing is a sublime way to learn to reflect and make something of your experiences-to "read" your own life as well as write about it.
5. In journal writing, process matter much more than achievement.
6. Revel in language. Rediscover it. Play with it and let it reveal new worlds to you.
7. Journal writing is unashamedly subjective, but while you are discovering what you really care about, the world around you will also become more interesting.
8. Retire the inner judge. Journal writing is for pleasure.

KEY HINTS

1. Combine your everyday recording of facts and impressions with exercises that will help you write and live more creatively.
2. Value the details. It's always the details that make the writing "yours".
3. Look forward as you write; no need to stop to criticize, edit, rewrite.
4. Add texture through the "additions" to your journal: sketches, drawings, quotations, ticket stubs, letter, poems, list, promises.

5. In your journal, you can never be too curious.
6. Writing things down clears the way for new insights.
7. Use all your senses.
8. Forget what you wrote yesterday or any another day. Come into this day, freshly.

Don't forget that you can argue on the page, take opposing or shifting viewpoints, write dialogue or poetry, and spend your "writing time" drawing. It is entirely up to you.

Journal Writing Exercises

- As you start: Note the date, time and place of your writing. *("Curled up on the sofa in my red and white pajamas". Softened by Mozart).
- Note your state of mind right now. ("Too many deadlines yet feeling at sweet peace...")
- Choose your number (between 1 and 111). That will give you your topic accept it!
- Take time to reflect on it. Let yourself drift.
- Write for at least twenty minutes.
- No stopping to edit or rewrite.
- End by finishing this sentence? "It was glorious to discover..."
- If you feel "unfinished," come back to the same topic within a day or so and patiently start all over again. Do so with a beginner's mind, as though this topic were entirely new to you.

Don't forget to choose a number, not a topic. Increase the element of challenge and surprise.

1. My life as a five-year-old.
2. My life as a ninety-five-year-old.
3. "I want to tell my younger self that..."

4. "The gifts that I can offer the world include…"
5. "Now that all my problems are solved I am free to…"
6. "What I value most about my life right now is…"
7. "I am now ready to look at…"
8. "My attitude to money comes from…"
9. "I have everything I need."
10. "What I want most is…"
11. "It's hard for me to say what I want."
12. "What I appreciate most about my gender/sexuality/age is…"
13. "My obituary."
14. "My ambitions."
15. "When I look at the world outside myself, I see that…"
16. "If my soul could speak, it would say…"
17. "People expect me to…"
18. "I give the impression that…"
19. "Becoming 'myself' would mean…"
20. "I am sorry about…"
21. "I am not sorry about…"
22. "The best way I know to get over a disappointment…"
23. "What life has taught me is that…"
24. "I feel most in tune with life and myself when…"
25. "I'd like to be more generous, but…"
26. "If I were a better person, I would…"
27. "To describe my creativity in less than two hundred words would…"
28. "The talent I would develop if I had half a chance is…"
29. "The qualities that other people admire in me are…"
30. "If other people could change me, they would want me to…"
31. "The way I most like to encourage myself and other people is…"
32. "The values I have chosen to live by are…"
33. "I can afford to be wrong about…"
34. A letter to someone no longer in my life.

35. A letter to someone you hurt.
36. A letter to someone who hurt you.
37. "The guiding principle of my life is…"
38. "I am not prejudiced, but…"
39. "I give most of my time to…"
40. "I hurt myself when…"
41. "I hurt others when…"
42. "If I dared to say what I really think…"
43. "The most crucial aspect of my identity is…"
44. "The principle I would stand up for is…"
45. "What I most appreciate about my life is…"
46. "My life surprises me…"
47. "The world is dangerous yet…"
48. "I can appreciate nature most when…"
49. "the thing about my own nature is…"
50. "I can't help…"
51. Life is a miracle.
52. "To me a miracle is…"
53. "Tough times have taught me that…"
54. "Loving deeply would mean…"
55. "I am deeply touched by…"
56. "I am supported by…"
57. "My life gets meaning from…"
58. "What I love most about my friends is…"
59. "What my friends love most about me…"
60. "No one knows that…"
61. "Retiring the inner critic means…"
62. "Letting perfection go, I can discover…"
63. "Pleasing others means…"
64. "Not pleasing others means…"
65. "For sheer pleasure I am going to write about…"
66. Unconditional love for me means…"

67. "What my most basic needs are…"
68. "My most basic needs are…"
69. "I have learned to live without…"
70. "I could live without…"
71. "I don't want to die without…"
72. "My children/friend/family will remember me for…"
73. "Other people's rules…"
74. "I am different from my parents in that…"
75. "I'd like to be different from my parents…"
76. "I am in charge of my own life…"
77. "I am writing this journal because…"
78. "Creativity matters to me more than anything…"
79. "I didn't get my fair share of creativity. Nevertheless…"
80. "I am making the most of what I have…"
81. "These are my limits…"
82. "I am most proud when…"
83. "My creativity is best expressed when…"
84. "I can see the goodness in…"
85. "I have the power to…"
86. "Thinking about it again, I…"
87. "I am fine as I am…"
88. "What I love about getting older is…"
89. "Five years ago I didn't know…"
90. "No one should have to suffer."
91. "I shouldn't have to suffer."
92. "I want to say no to…"
93. Friendship
94. Gratitude
95. Write a letter of thanks
96. Write a letter of appreciation to someone who annoys you.
97. Write a letter of appreciation to yourself.
98. "The bad habit I am ready to jettison is…"

99. "Starting from today I can…"

100. Food.

101. Food for the soul.

102. When I think about making my environment more beautiful…"

103. Sharing what I have.

104. "I need to forgive…"

105. I need to ask _____ to forgive me…"

106. "What I appreciate most about my body is…"

107. "If I had all the time in the world, I would…"

108. "I am totally inspired by…"

109. "I am moved by…"

110. "Every time I think about joy…"

111. "Journal writing is giving me…"

HOW OTHERS EXPERIENCED MY STORM

I asked my family, caretakers and good friends who were there for me during the thick of my struggle to answer certain questions. It is my hope that their feedback below will serve as a reference for others whose loved ones are struggling.

FAMILY

Kennedy Kantor (age 9-12 at the time):

Explain what this experience was like for you. What was the worst part, best part, what did you learn from it. How did it impact your life?

The experience was interesting to say the least. My mom wasn't really able to be a part of our family. She could not participate in anything. She'd just lie around on the couch, in agony. Thankfully, my dad, brothers, aunts and uncles took care of me. The worst part of my mom's situation was seeing her cry all the time, and her not being able to fully function. That was hard for me to deal with. I was worried that she would die and would not be around to see me grow up. It was also hard for me not to have my mom be who she used to be - the bubbly, playful, loving, silly caretaker mom that I had always known. The best part, if there was a best part, was laying in my bed and talking, bonding and laughing with my mom, and I also loved playing games with her and my brothers and dad, like cards and Shopkins. She would laugh really hard when I would act out the

Shopkins' personalities. I learned that we just have to take each day, one day at at time, and be in the present moment. That is all we ever have. It's important to focus on what we do have. I learned to really enjoy our family time together and not to take anything for granted. Enjoy each moment. The experience made me stronger and made me more independent. I had to learn how to do a lot of things for myself, which made me who I am today. I wasn't even resentful that I had to do things for myself that my mom would otherwise do for me. I just rolled with the punches and grew up as I had to at the time. I didn't think much of it. It was just my life. Maybe it was because I was nine and I didn't really know that there was any other way. I was sad for my mom, but I was also nine, so I didn't really know what else to do but handle the situation as best I could, by being the fun-loving nine-year-old that I was and trying constantly to cheer her up. With a sick mother and three guys around who didn't really understand anything about being a young girl, I did not fully get to live that carefree life of being a kid in my own home. Luckily, I had my aunties and cousins, and I would go over to their houses, where I could be a regular nine-year-old kid.

How did this situation impact your relationships with your parents/siblings/spouse?

I got closer with my older brothers during that time. My oldest brother Sammy, especially, would always check in with me and ask me how I was doing. He made extra efforts to make sure that I was OK. When I wasn't feeling well, he was there for me. One time I got sick and threw up, and he cleaned it up. That's love. I'm sure that was the only time my mom was happy that she couldn't move off the couch. My dad stepped in and became Mr. Mom. He took me to school, to activities and to my friends' houses. We became closer because of the time I got to spend with him.

What advice would you give someone who has a family member who is struggling?

For anyone who has a family member who is struggling, the advice I would give them would be to think positively and believe that their loved one will get better. Also, distraction is key! Play games and try to uplift that family member, and distract them from their situation. Believe that everything will be okay. Also, no matter how old you are when you are experiencing a tragedy, try as hard as it may be to remember how old you are and that you have to live your own life, too. Surround yourself with friends and family members. Don't lose yourself in another's tragedy.

And, when all else fails, go to your aunt's house... that's what I did!

Nate Kantor (age 12-15 at the time):

Explain what this experience was like for you... Worst part, best part, what you learned from it, how it impacted your life...?

As a young kid, around the age of twelve with your typical, underwhelming amount of emotional strength, this experience was debilitating, tear-jerking and arduously navigated. It was confusing for me to go day by day without having the support of my mother, but instead, having to instead support her. I remember the worst part of it all most vividly, so I'll begin with that. Of course, it wouldn't be as dramatic without darkness and rain; and it was just that, a dark and rainy night. Dark because my mother couldn't handle light; the rain, just depressingly coincidental. It was just me and my mother, shortly before my father had arrived home from work. I was in my room. I heard her door open, followed by the groan of each demanding step she took. She typically didn't walk out of her room, but this time she walked downstairs. I figured maybe she had gained some motivation to get some food or water by herself. I listened intently to the sounds coming from below. After no familiar sounds registered, like the flow of water from the jug, or the magnetic release of the refrigerator, I decided to investigate.

I saw her standing in the kitchen in front of the knife drawer. "Just do it, just do it", she whispered. I rushed over and calmly removed the knife from her hand, whispering, "Let's *not* do that." The knife was pointed away from her, as if she wanted to, but knew she couldn't. As I write this now at nineteen, it feels like I'm remembering a movie I saw years ago. It doesn't feel real. Perhaps it's the result of some traumatic defense mechanism used by the psyche of my younger self, and current self. I walked her back upstairs and sat with her until my dad got home. I didn't tell my dad about it that night; it was probably the last thing he wanted to hear after a long day's work. Looking back, had I not been immersed in these circumstances for a while prior to this experience, my behavior in its presence would have been much more unstable, and could have worsened the situation.

My mother's constant search for relief seemed everlasting. It was a never-ending debate about what route should be taken to optimize her healing process. Initially, she took a more holistic and naturopathic approach - as that is how my family typically approached health, using homeopathic or naturopathic remedies. They didn't help enough. The injury that my mother's brain had sustained could not be fixed by a remedy made of dolphin tears. It was more complex, and needed many years to heal. I remember fantasizing to myself that I would somehow discover the "cure" to my mother's ailment, and be the hero who ended her suffering.

I remember the good moments too - the ones that gave me and my family hope. After many different attempts with different medications, my mother would come across ones that would give her spurts of relief. One day in eighth grade, I reported to the back of the school where my brother would pick me up. This was the routine for most of middle school. But on this special day, I instead saw my mother in the big GMC, waving and smiling with so much joy. She was excited to pick me up. It was a blissful moment. I had hope that things were starting to turn around, that I was getting my mother back. That moment in particular changed a lot about me. It made me hyper-aware of other people's happiness, and when people aren't happy as well. It made me care more about the times when people are joyful, and to enjoy those fleeting moments. It made me immune to the little bothersome happenings of everyday life, and appreciate the little positives more. This whole experience made me who I am today, and for that I am grateful. However, there were ugly habits that were created as well.

Marijuana and I were a dangerous combo, more so to myself than to others. I like to say that weed found me, not the other way around. Regardless, I enjoyed the hell out of it. You could even say I was a full-blown pothead. Of course, I now know that it was a means to escape my emotions - to escape my situation. In that respect, my use of weed wasn't healthy. I knew I needed to stop, but quitting wasn't easy. I had become addicted, as such my father had to intervene. I thought I was slick, but blowing smoke out the window somehow doesn't mean it's not getting in the house. My father would recognize the smell and immediately bombard my pot ridden room. After a good dozen *aha moments*, it eventually came to an end. On the other hand, pot did lead me down some positive paths. Philosophy and yogic practices are just two of the things that I believe I found because of marijuana. Weed allowed me to think more clearly about just one thing. It allowed me to explore aspects of my life that I never knew existed, all while hiding me from the emotions brought about by my family's circumstances.

How did this situation impact your relationships with your parents/siblings/spouse?

There were many instances where I wasn't sure how to react to what was going on. I would analyze my brother mostly, to see and embody the way that he was reacting. My little sister would do that exact same thing with both me and my brother. I was somewhat aware of her reliance on both of us, though sometimes I wouldn't care, and we would argue and bicker as normal. The biggest change in dynamic was my relationship with my father. All at once four people became immensely reliant on him. I couldn't imagine how this would have felt. He had no one to look to for support in our household, which is why I am so grateful we have an incredible extended family. They supported us and my father through the whole thing. I'm not sure we would have gotten through it without them.

What advice would you give someone who has a family member who is struggling?

The biggest take-away from all this is to be aware of your own happiness, and the happiness of those around you. Frolic in those moments and don't take them for granted.

Sammy Kantor (age 14-17 at the time):

Explain what this experience was like for you. What was the worst part, best part, what did you learn from it. How did it impact your life?

My mom's experience was very traumatizing, but it also made me a much more empathetic person. Her struggle did have an impact on me as a teen. I couldn't just be free and not care about anything like the average teenager in my community. I did have something to care about. Her tragedy was happening during my freshman, sophomore and junior years of high school. I feel like I blocked out a lot of it. The first year and a half, my mom was in bed all the time. I would go to school, come home, and just go upstairs to say hi to her. I would always hear her crying... it sucked to hear my mom wailing in so much agony. It sucked, but since it was happening all the time, I came to a place where I decided - this is happening, this is how it is, and I don't want to be depressed about it. I used to try to console her by playing cards and other games with her. I'd try anything I could to distract her from her pain. I guess it kind of helped both of us, really. I got her to stop crying for a while, and she got to stop crying for a while. I was really busy because I played soccer. I had practice three times per week and games on weekends, so I had something else to focus on other than the situation at home with my mom. I took my soccer commitment as a welcomed distraction and just went with it. Two years in, my mom was at that phase where she really wanted to give up on life. She played me a recording that she made of herself pouring out her feelings and her love for me. She had me listen to it, explaining that when she was gone, I could play the recording to remember her. That was the first time I cried during the entire situation. I was very upset and couldn't stop crying, so my dad called my aunt, who is a therapist, to come talk to me. I needed help to get through that one. The other worst experience I had was when my dad cried in front of me. He is usually very stoic and does not show his vulnerability or his feelings. One night, he just broke down in front of me. That was brutal. He started crying and hugging me. He was being vulnerable, so I felt that I had to be strong. I just hugged him back and was there for him, but I was crying inside, too.

The best part of the long ordeal was when my mom returned from Menninger and she *smiled* for the first time in three years. A genuine smile. That was the best. I learned so much from the experience. Empathy and sympathy, mainly. I also learned that life is too short.

I learned a lot about myself, too. I learned that I was stronger than I ever knew. Having to rise up and take care of my two younger siblings and be there emotionally for my parents made me realize that I could handle anything that life threw my way, with strength, and not let the tragedy take me down a negative path. I took on responsibility as it came. I feel like I still led a good life during the challenging time. I didn't let my family situation stop me from living out my high school experience. I really did have a great high school experience. I did sometimes feel guilty when I would go out and leave my family at home, but my parents were really supportive and talked to me about living my life and continuing to be a kid and to have my experiences. It was a bummer for me that none of my family members were ever at my soccer games, but I understood completely.

How did this situation impact your relationships with your parents/ siblings/spouse?

My mom and I became a lot closer. We talked a lot and bonded during that time. I bonded a lot with my siblings and dad, too. We had to be there for each other, which brought us closer. I was the "extra parent." I helped my sister, Kennedy, with her homework, and whenever she was sick and needed care. Plus, I drove my brother, Nate, to his friends' houses. I never did any of the grocery shopping or anything like that, but I felt like the extra parent, nonetheless, doing the other things an adult would normally do for a child.

What advice would you give someone who has a family member who is struggling?

The advice I would give someone in my same situation is to never give up on their loved one. Never give up on your family, especially during such a challenging time. Always stay positive and look to the bright side. Even though there will be shitty times in life, we can choose to stay positive and hopeful.

Doron Kantor (age - brown hair to grey hair):

Explain what this experience was like for you... Worst part, best part, what you learned from it, how it impacted your life...?

The experience was very painful to watch, seeing my wife struggle like that. I couldn't understand how she continued to regress for three long years. It was very difficult to witness the side of her that nobody else saw, only myself and our kids. She would put on a very big front when people would come to visit, but when we were alone, we saw the hell she was in, displayed right in front of us - the pain and suffering. I had to watch my practice decrease in production up to seventy percent. We had caretakers but they found it difficult to watch Joelle experience so much discomfort. Every single one of them eventually said they couldn't stand it and couldn't watch it any longer. When we had exhausted all of our resources, she started talking about the end being imminent... if she could not find any normalcy. She talked about the fact that she would handle taking her own life if it had to come to that, and that she would take care of the details. She felt that she couldn't handle the pain any longer, and she wanted to be in a better place, relieved of her suffering. That was very difficult to hear, but to be quite honest, the kids and I talked about it, and we all understood, even at their young ages... we all came to realize that their mother may not be with us anymore, if she could not find relief. They understood that she would be at peace which was what we all wanted for her... preferably with us. The pain and suffering was so intense in her state. It was very hard to understand why my wife was put through what she was put through. She believes there is a reason for everything, and that it's all from "God," but I could not understand why any loving deity would allow her to go through that. The scariest part of it was when I was driving her to the emergency room during one of her very bad episodes, and she opened the car door and attempted to jump out of the car while we were speeding down the freeway. I held her back in the car, pulled over to the shoulder of the freeway and called an ambulance. I didn't know what the outcome of the situation would be. I hoped she would not take her own life. My friends who watched me going through this would often ask me, "How can you put up with this? How can you deal with your wife like this?" Then they'd say, "I would never be able to go through what you're going through. I would have to leave." I told them that I made a commitment to someone and that I was going to spend the rest of my life with her. I was not going to leave her in her most critical time of need, or ever. The worst part was watching the lack of support from some of the most important people in Joelle's life, when she needed them most. Many crucial people did not really ever reach out to find out how we were all doing. It was very disheartening. Their attitude appeared to be that if we needed something, we could reach out. That was disappointing to me. And, thinking that I may not be able to spend the rest of my life with the person who I wanted to spend the rest of my life with was devastating. Marriage is the hardest job in the world. But in the end, I've always had the desire to be with Joelle over anyone else. She accepts all of me and I accept all of her. We are each other's partners for life. I could not imagine being with anyone else, so the thought of losing her was really painful.

The best part of the three years of hell was when I realized Joelle was definitely improving. In addition to all the natural remedies she tried, we found a medication that brought her enough relief for her to slowly start to engage in life again. It took six months of constant improvements to realize Joelle was truly on the mend. Her pain and her suffering were improving weekly. She was healing and we now understood that life would return to our version of normal once again.

Another positive part of this was witnessing how my children handled the situation. They learned never to give up and never to let go: they saw me hold on through a very challenging time. My kids learned to keep moving forward, keep striving, keep going. I am grateful that our situation finally took a turn for the better.

The other thing that I experienced was true friendship. I learned who my true friends were and who really cared and was willing to be there for us. I don't tolerate bullshit anymore. I have no time for a front. I have no time for people who are not who they say they are. I would rather have one solid friend in my life than fifty superficial friends. I learned that about people and about myself.

How did this situation impact your relationships with your parents/ siblings/spouse?

It impacted my relationship with my parents and siblings in a positive way. They were all generously supportive to Joelle and me, and especially to our kids. My family has always been very tight. We left South Africa as a family and remained connected in America. We have always been very close and very supportive of each other. In regards to my children, I am a very proud father. No parent is perfect... I'm certainly not. But when push came to shove, each of them individually pulled through like incredible stars. My daughter at nine-years-old entertained my wife. Our son Samuel spent hours lying with his mom when she needed the support. It was hardest for Nathan to deal with, but he still came through and supported his mom when I was fried. I grew to respect and have such great admiration for my kids with all that they went through and how they handled our situation and persevered.

I've always been committed to Joelle in marriage and fidelity. This situation gave me a new respect for my wife in terms of her strength and perseverance. I admire her for the battle she endured and the way she fought for her survival. I am very honored to have been part of her journey and to watch her succeed.

What advice would you give someone who has a family member who is struggling?

Give my wife a call!

FRIENDS

Heather Taylor:

1. Explain what this situation was like for you?
(worst part, best part, what you learned from it, how it impacted you).

It was very hard for me to see Joelle's anguish and inability to function. I know she felt helpless, but I also felt that way, and it was truly sad. It was as if she were in an altered state all the time, not in the same world as the rest of us. It was hard to grasp how to help her, which made it challenging simply to sit by. Like everyone who loves her, I wanted to know *how* to FIX IT?! And after a long period of all the different treatments, specialists, etc., wondering how or if her issues would ever get solved became a very scary prospect. Primarily, the impact on me was just that it hurt my heart, and I ached for her. Joelle had been my best friend for almost thirty years when she sustained her fourth brain injury. We have always been close, so her being in so much agony was something that weighed heavily on me. Joelle's situation showed me how life can just change in an instant without any warning. It also taught me not to take anything for granted - health, especially.

2. How did this situation impact your personal life? Relationships with your family members?

Joelle's struggle gave my family something to discuss. We talked about how unwanted and unforeseen experiences can occur in life, and how we just have to take them as they come, as best we can.

We also recognized how blessed we were that our family was not dealing with a similar situation, as I know how hard it was for Doron and the kids to go through that experience with Joelle. I just kept expressing to the kids and my husband how fragile we all are. It was very impactful when I traveled with Joelle to Florida to get her settled at the Hippocrates Health Institute. She struggled tremendously trying to overcome all of the stimulation in the airport. Getting her on the plane, then having to fly across the country was just a huge endeavor for her. That whole process and the week that followed were important to me. I was so grateful I was the person that could be there to support her and also go through the experience with her. I was deeply touched to be the "caregiver" in that process.

3. What advice would you give someone who has a family member or loved one who is deeply struggling?

That is a tough one! Each situation is so unique. I guess I would say that the best thing anyone can do is just be supportive and caring. Especially when you cannot do anything to solve it, the next best thing is to be consistent with care, support and patience.

Connie Sadis:

Joelle, you are one of the most optimistic, "look on the bright side, and if that doesn't work, try this" woman... I know. So, your descent came as a shock to me. I kept thinking that at any moment the "real" Joelle would re-emerge.

You were living on a fault line and I so badly wanted to say, "just step over the line, you can do it." For me, the hardest part of this time in your life was watching your intense struggles and pure desperation. Your phone calls of hyperventilating panic attacks, crying in agony, and worse yet, hearing you surrender to the fervent agony, sent me driving over to your house in haste to be with you. Regrettably, there wasn't anything I could do to take the pain away and that left me feeling helpless and extremely sad.

It seems that you wanted so much for those of us who were trying to help you to see and feel through your prism/lens, what "it" felt like, describing a "buzzy" feeling. We would walk, and walk, and walk, as a means of distraction. I would try to suggest conversation ideas or try to make you laugh, but the only way to describe your interaction would be complete emptiness.

While walking, we would reflect on your past and on the incidents that deeply wounded you… did those circumstances interplay with your current condition? And if so, were they the root cause or were they emotional tragedies, buried under years of peril, emerging amongst the weeds of your struggle?

You tried so many remedies, earnestly seeking help. Our drives to Steve's chiropractic office in Issaquah were memorable for me. Steve had a new instrument that he was convinced would help you. While waiting for your appointment we wondered, do we wait in the car or do we risk going into the office where undoubtedly someone would be wearing a scent too strong for your fatigued senses? The chiropractor in Burien had his own unique healing protocol. We'd wait in a dark room because lights exacerbated your "buzzy" feelings. There was also the cranial sacral person in Lynnwood who tried to alleviate your irritation and discomfort.

We went together on numerous visits to the hyperbaric chambers. Then, there was Terry, the specialty eye person. Would her tools be the answer? You took blood tests to try to figure out if your genetics were to blame. Could it have been the MTHFR gene or the way you processed vitamin D? Vitamin protocols, food sources, and marijuana… you tried so many avenues, only to come to so many dead ends. Sleep was imperative to your healing, but it alluded you many nights, which in turn multiplied the severity of the negative effects you experienced. The unknown was so hard. I greatly admired your fortitude in the face of so many disappointments.

We wondered if the surgery my neighbor Karen (who had suffered a concussion), went through to open the pathway for fluid to the brain would work for you. You took yourself on a getaway at a place in Kenmore to try to just experience some semblance of peace and get some space from your situation. Then, I was relieved that you finally found the place that helped you in Texas, Menninger.

It was hard hearing you cry in desperation about not being there for your sweet children, Kennedy, Nate and Sam. I would try to reason with you that your health situation was no different than any other mom who was dealing with something like cancer, and not able to support her kids through the recovery process. I would remind you that you were blessed with sisters-in-law who were the next best thing to a mom. But the torment you felt about not being there for your kids was palpable.

Picking Kenna up from school, taking her out for frozen yogurt, and spending time with her allowed me to see how it was affecting her. She was so strong during the process, yet as any eleven-year-old would ponder, she said, "They tell me what a hard time mom is having, but what about me?" I was proud of her for using her voice and discussing her needs.

I remember hurting for you while witnessing the acute sadness you experienced when some friends lacked support for you during this difficult time.

To give your family a "break" or if Doron had to go to work, I'd pick you up to bring you to my house. You were in such a bad state that Doron worried about you being by yourself, and I believe you were afraid to be alone. I recall perceiving that you did not want to die, but I was concerned that the pain was so uncomfortable and intense that it hurt to live.

The symptoms you felt were so distressing that you had a hard time remembering things.

You would repeat yourself often and forget topics that we had discussed. Even in the midst of your recovery, you would repeat yourself often. I was always okay with that because it was just awesome to see you wanting to communicate, especially with less strain.

Your situation did not impact my personal relationships. My family felt sad for you. They were happy to help on the days you came over (wearing no lotions or perfume, lights off, minimal noise, and having no candles burning, of course). You would sit in my living room or lie on the couch on my deck, willing the pain to go away.

Even in the darkest of days, I could sense your hope and desire to heal. You spoke of your favorite things… hearts and rainbows. You reflected on the simple things in life that you would never take for granted again, like going to a movie. You dreamed of the car that you would drive… a white BMW.

You were a fighter during all of this, and I am sooooo proud of you and your healing!!!

The advice I would give to someone going through any struggle is to try all the remedies possible because every millimeter of hope is still hope. Trying any remedy or protocol keeps that hope alive. I cannot help but think that perhaps the cumulative effect of all that you tried, Joelle, is what brought you to *your* healing point. I would also recommend to just be emotionally and physically present for anyone who is struggling in your life. Catch them when they fall. Encourage their healing and listen to their heartaches.

Ana Proctor:

1. Explain what this situation was like for you - (worst part, best part, what you learned from it, how it impacted you).

I really got to know Joelle around the time of her fall. We bonded almost immediately, as we shared a similar experience of being sensitive souls trying to navigate what feels like an insensitive world. I had a newborn at the time and was beginning to feel the difficult effects of postpartum depression. Navigating the trenches on my own was not only isolating, but it came with the feeling of being seen as broken, incompetent, crazy, strange, etc. Even with family and friends doing their best to offer support, those individuals cannot fully relate to where I was in life, and their capacity for understanding could only go so far. Joelle and I had the blessing, or maybe divine timing, of being in the trenches together. We would take turns picking each other up when the other was too weary, offering consolation and the powerful yet simple shoulder to cry on. Through our experience, we were able to provide each other with the wisdom and advice that only another who sees the darkness can provide. At the end of the day, my experience watching Joelle navigate her journey was very much a blessing in disguise. I believe a higher power made sure each one of us had a Guardian Angel to light the way.

2. How did this situation impact your personal life? Relationships with your family members?

This was a time in my life where having a friend to confide in was crucial. Sharing wisdom and advice through such a dark time with someone I trusted solidified that, in fact, we were having a human experience. I loved how our kids bonded and we bonded with each other's kids. There is something special about the family you get to choose. I think for Joelle and me, we got to choose each other and also to practice boundaries, which is something we did not grow up with. I think the experience with Joelle had a profound effect on my relationship with my own family and how I choose the relationships in my life.

3. What advice would you give someone who has a family member or loved one who is deeply struggling?

For those out there finding it difficult to support a loved one who is struggling, I urge you to look at your relationship in a completely different way. If you cannot relate with someone who is experiencing difficulty, it is so important to remember that you are not responsible for "fixing" that person. Many times, what is happening is an opportunity for you to look into areas of your life that you have been avoiding, and learn to move through your own feelings. Empathy is sitting and listening. Observing, not judging. You can offer help and support, and many times that might not be taken, but you can still offer it. It's important to know when to move back and allow the person in agony to have their own experience, no matter how adamant you are about "knowing" what they need to do. You cannot expect to understand what someone is going through if you have not trudged through similar waters. Taking care of yourself is also crucial while trying to care for others. The person who is struggling may come out differently at the other end of their struggle. They may likely be different than who they were to you before. Support them where they are, even if they have to move in a different direction.

CARETAKERS

Kelly Hudson:

The hardest part of the experience was observing the pain and uncertainty on the faces of her family, especially her husband. It was devastating at times to see what Joelle was experiencing. What I was able to see was how very much Doron loves Joelle, and how he would have moved mountains to help her.

I spent a lot of time with Joelle through her journey and it was personally very much an eye-opener for me. It reminded me to be thankful for my health and my family, and allowed me to view how others deal with pain and suffering, both mental and physical. It showed me how victory over adversity is possible. Another thing I learned is the importance of being your own advocate, and of having others there to advocate for you until you are fully heard and understood. Be annoying, be persistent, be a pest in the ear of whomever will listen, even when they won't. The answer is out there somewhere, so you just need to keep fighting for it.

Personally, the entire process created an intense feeling of responsibility for the whole family. Whether they know it or not, I see them as an extended part of my family. I would do anything for any of them.

I learned that you should never give up, that the answer could be just one more step around the corner, that even when you are face-down in the worst of it, there could always be a solution that you have not tried. Be open to all things, listen to your gut, and keep trying to find a solution. Never give up hope. Sometimes surrender means being open to options that were previously considered closed off or impossible. In a situation where literally your life is on the line, forget pride. There is no room for that. Ask for help from whomever you can get it, and just be thankful that you are still alive. Just keep moving forward.

Abby Lodmer:

Explain what this experience was like for you... Worst part, best part, what you learned from it, how it impacted your life...?

Helping to care for Joelle during her time of great struggle was a privilege for which I will be forever grateful. I learned so much about the fragility of human life and about health and healing, by spending great chunks of time with Joelle for a few months during her horrible situation. I happily agreed to be Joelle's health coach and main daytime caretaker, and to help her heal as best I could with everything I had in my toolbelt... but her head injury and the devastating effects of it were something that I had never experienced in my almost twenty years of helping people heal themselves of chronic and catastrophic dis-eases and dis-orders. The worst part for me was the constant feeling I had that I was standing helplessly by, while Joelle suffered so intensely. No amount of positive affirmations, hugs, sprouts, green juice, treatments by renowned healers or herbal tinctures alleviated her ailments in any sizable way. All of those who cared for Joelle throughout those three years experienced great frustration, because nothing they/we did seemed to help her predicament. Joelle, herself, experienced the greatest level of frustration as she suffered through her traumatic brain injury, as she was not quite sure what it was at the time, nor did she know how long it would take to heal. Her total vulnerability and desperation was heart-wrenching to witness, though her strength, courage and determination to try *every* healing modality without giving up on herself, was deeply inspiring. If I were in the same amount of constant pain, I don't know if I could have lived with it, especially not for *three years*. But Joelle pushed through and held on until she found some modicum of relief. Being able to witness Joelle's willingness to try anything to help herself, and her level of fortitude even in the depths of hell, were inspiring beyond words. I am a better person and a more empathetic health coach for my clients because of Joelle.

How did this situation impact your relationships with your parents/siblings/spouses?

Working with Joelle through her crisis helped me to put things into perspective. Being that close to someone who was experiencing that level of misery made me want to celebrate my own functional body and mind, and to remain in a state of gratitude for all that I did have going right in my life, like my relationship with my now husband.

What advice would you give someone who has a family member who is struggling?

Joelle taught me so much about how to really be there for someone in need. That is the advice I would give someone who has a loved one who is struggling - just *be* there for them. Let them know you are there for them, even if you can only be there for them in a limited capacity. Check in and ask the person who is struggling how he/she/they would like for you to show up for them. People need to know that they are supported and thought about, especially during challenging times. I would also say to be honest about your limitations and availability. Be supportive and up front.

Michelle Romero:

Joelle's husband, Dr. Kantor, is my chiropractor. One day, while meeting him for an adjustment, he approached me, knowing that I have a background in caregiving, and asked me to help assist in caring for his wife. I naturally accepted, as I love helping people. Over the period of several months, I accompanied Joelle to several different specialists, including an integrative medicine expert, a naturopathic physician, a chiropractor specializing in neurology, and a colored-tinted lenses specialist (Irlen Method). I also sat through multiple sessions in a hyperbaric chamber with her and helped her seek out different modalities of healing to help relieve some of her symptoms and the uneasiness she constantly felt. I cooked for her, cleaned for her, shopped for her, ran errands for her and cried for her. I did all I could to help her and her family.

Having gone to all of those specialists with Joelle, I learned quite a lot about health and healing, which was very helpful to me and my family, and for that I am grateful. The most difficult part for me was seeing Joelle suffer, while there was *nothing* I could do about it. It was very difficult for an empath like me to not be able to bring some relief or comfort to someone I cared about. At times, she was managing, at other times she seemed like she was possessed by something beyond her control, in all the pain she was in. All the while, I stayed for support and unconditional love to her and her family as much as I could.

The experience I received while working with Joelle taught me many things about myself and my family. For example, after sitting in with her at her neurologist appointments and learning about Spect Brain Imaging, I discovered that not only did I have ADD, but my son and daughter also had the disorder, which explained their difficulties in school. I was able to get support for my kids, but more importantly, I learned to give them grace and also give myself grace.

The advice I would give someone who is dealing with a loved one who is deeply struggling is to remember that the person they know and love is in there, beyond the pain, and to be patient. Our God is a God of compassion. He doesn't love us *if* we do something or *when* we do something else. He loves us *just because*. His love is unconditional. That is how we should love one another.

People who struggle with brain injuries and depression are just as important and significant as those who may be struggling with another, more visible injury. Their battle is not only their own. It affects those who love them as well. Supporting someone with mental anguish is very difficult. Self-care is also crucial when caring for someone in distress. Self-care is not selfish; in fact, it's vital.

Each day that we wake up we are given the gift of time. What we do with that gift is our choice. We can choose to love one another without conditions, or we can be selfish, self-centered and without empathy. I choose to live life by serving others, to the best of my ability. I am grateful for the time I got to spend with Joelle.

Printed in the United States
by Baker & Taylor Publisher Services